HIKING THE
Highest Passes of
C·O·L·O·R·A·D·O

Bob Martin

PRUETT PUBLISHING COMPANY
BOULDER, COLORADO

Library of Congress Cataloging-in-Publication Data

Martin, Bob, 1920-
    Hiking the highest passes.
    Includes index.
    1. Hiking—Colorado—Guide-books. 2. Mountain passes—Colorado—Guide-books. 3. Colorado—Description and travel—1981— —Guide-books. I. Title
GV199.42.C6M365 1984 917.88 84-6893
ISBN 0-87108-756-1 (pbk.)

Second Edition
  2 3 4 5 6 7 8 9

Printed in the United States of America.
Cover design by Cover to Cover Design, Denver, Colorado.

Contents

Introduction

Hike Destinations

Trailhead Data

State Map Showing Hike Locations

Rocky Mountain National Park and
  Indian Peaks Wilderness Hikes

Front Range and Gore Range Hikes

Sawatch Range and Sangre de Cristo Range Hikes

Elk Mountain Hikes

San Juan Mountain Hikes

All photos by author except as noted.

Introduction

Hiking to a high pass can be more dramatic than hiking to a lake or climbing a mountain. The reason is that the panorama on the other side of the pass unfolds all at once. In a sense, the secrets are withheld so that the anticipation of what may be on the other side builds to a climax for that moment when the pass is reached.

In our many years of hiking together in Colorado, my wife Dotty climbed most of the fourteen-thousand-foot peaks with me. When she decided that she didn't want to attempt to climb several of the hardest Fourteeners, she proposed an alternative: "Why not try to hike to all of Colorado's highest passes?" We decided to do just that, but we needed a reference that listed the passes by elevation so that we could determine a reasonable goal. That's how this book came into being.

There are many books on Colorado's mountain passes, most of which approach the subject from a historical standpoint or describe some of the passes that can be reached by automobile. However, none have listed all of the high passes by elevation or explained how to get to the ones that cannot be reached by automobile.

After much research, and with the help of some special tabulations made by the United States Board on Geographic Names, we developed data on all of Colorado's named passes. When arranged in order of elevation, there are sixty passes twelve thousand feet and above. These seemed to make a reasonable hiking and climbing goal.

It turns out that only sixteen of these sixty highest passes in Colorado can be reached by automobile. The other forty-four are best reached on foot, some by easy walks, others by long hikes, and a few by more difficult hiking and climbing.

Surprisingly, almost all of the forty-four passes above twelve thousand feet that cannot be reached by automobile make fine hikes. In this book we describe a hiking route to each of these forty-four passes. In addition to the routes to the highest passes, we have included six other route descriptions to passes above eleven thousand feet that we believe make excellent hikes.

Passes and Peaks Compared

After having been to all sixty of the state's twelve-thousand-foot passes, we've found some remarkable similarities to climbing the fourteen-thousand-foot peaks. A few of the high mountains and passes can be reached or approached very closely by automobile. Like the Fourteeners, some of the high passes are easy walks, and some are strenuous all-day treks. Others are off-trail routes on difficult terrain. Also, like the Fourteeners, a few of the high passes are remote enough to require backpacking.

Geographically, the 12,000-foot passes are found generally in the same areas as the Fourteeners, but there are some interesting differences. Rocky Mountain National Park has one Fourteener and seven of the high passes. The Mosquito Range has five Fourteeners but only one of the high passes. The Elk Mountains, with six Fourteeners, has fourteen of the high passes. Several high passes are in areas with no Fourteeners—the Gore Range, the West Elk Mountains, and the southeastern part of the San Juan Mountains.

There is one major difference between climbing all of the Fourteeners and reaching all of the twelve-thousand-foot passes. There are no high passes that are as difficult to reach as the summits of some Fourteeners. Therefore, reaching all of the twelve-thousand-foot passes is a reasonable goal for many more people. We think that this goal is every bit as interesting and satisfying as climbing all of the Fourteeners. We hope that this book will inspire many others to share our experiences.

Using the Route Descriptions

At the beginning of each hike description, tabular information gives a brief overview of the hike.

The **elevation** of each pass from the latest United States Geological Survey map is shown first in the data introducing each route description.

The **hiking distance** is the total distance to reach the pass and return to the trailhead on the route covered in the description. The route described is considered practical and enjoyable for hiking to the pass and is not always the shortest possible hiking route.

The **starting elevation** is shown for the beginning point of the hike.

The **elevation gain** is the amount of climbing that is required to hike to the pass and return to the starting point. It is at least as great as the difference between the starting elevation and the elevation of the pass. The elevation gain usually is more than that difference, since most routes have some descents along the ascent route.

The **rating** is intended to give a general idea of the difficulty of the hike. **Easy** hikes usually are short ones all on trail or on readily walked cross-country routes. **Moderate** hikes may involve some steep slopes and/or boulder hopping, or may be longer hikes on trail. **Difficult** hikes may require rock scrambling, bushwhacking, maneuvering steeper slopes, or route finding or may be extremely long. These ratings are only intended to divide the hikes in this book into groups. Some experienced hikers might consider all of these hikes to be easy, while beginning hikers may have difficulty completing some of the hikes rated to be easy.

The **estimated time** gives a general idea of how long it will take to complete the hike. It is based on continuous walking at a moderate pace, with brief rests and time for lunch. While speeds vary widely among different hikers, these estimated times are fairly consistent with one another. After you have taken several of these hikes, you can see whether your pace is faster or slower than the estimated times listed. Thus, you can better estimate your own time for subsequent hikes.

The **maps** listed are the United States Geological Survey topographic maps and United States Department of Agriculture Forest Service maps that apply to the route. The USGS maps are the 7.5 minute series, which are now available for all of these hikes.

The national forest maps are suggested for general orientation. They cover a wide area but do not show topography. National forest maps are most helpful for getting to the trailhead and for picking out distant landmarks. These maps cover territory well beyond the forest boundary and often are useful even though the hike may not be within a national forest.

The USGS topographic maps, beyond the portions included in this book, are particularly suggested for the off-trail hikes and for some of the longer trail hikes. Such maps are good to have on even the easiest hikes since they show so much interesting detail. A USGS topographic map covering all of Rocky Mountain National Park provides general orientation for that area.

Trail Signs

Our hiking directions are prepared without reference to trail signs. Unfortunately, many trail signs are stolen, moved, or destroyed by vandals. Undoubtedly, you will find some trail signs on many of these routes. However, we don't feel that the chance of them being there when you make the trip is great enough for you to rely on them. Therefore, we suggest that you try to become well oriented with regard to direction, landmarks, and physical features so that trail signs aren't necessary for you to find your way.

Choosing A Hike

Hikes to the high passes are best made in the summer

hiking season—June through October. All of them begin at a trailhead that can be reached by passenger car under good conditions.

The table "Hike Destinations" (which follows this Introduction) lists the objectives that can be reached on the hikes in this book. For each hike, a high pass is the final destination. Lakes and other intermediate objectives along the way also are listed. If the hike all the way to the pass cannot be completed, these intermediate objectives often make a suitable alternate destination.

The table "Trailhead Data" (which follows "Hike Destinations") can be helpful in selecting hikes. Used along with the state map showing hike locations, this table will locate the hikes most convenient for you.

For each hike, the trailhead and its elevation are shown. The next column shows distance to the nearest forest service or other governmental campground, if there is one closer than the nearest town. The distance to the nearest town that is large enough to have motels, food, and supplies is shown.

The next to last column shows the one-way distance that must be driven on unpaved roads to reach the trailhead. The final column shows the approximate number of miles the hike could be shortened, if any, by using a four-wheel-drive vehicle under optimum conditions along the route of the hike.

In many cases a good one-way hike can be worked out if suitable transportation arrangements can be made. The hike descriptions indicate many such possibilities. The hikes as described do not include any one-way hikes because of the vast distances between trailheads for many good one-way hikes and the inability of most hikers to arrange suitable transportation.

Reaching All Colorado High Passes

If you want to reach all sixty Colorado passes twelve thousand feet and above, there are sixteen more passes to visit in addition to the forty-four hikes included in this book. These passes can be reached or approached closely by automobile. Appendix 2 briefly describes the location and routes to these passes. If you're an avid hiker, you may prefer to hike rather than drive to some of these sixteen passes.

You may wish to consult some of the source books on driving to Colorado passes. One of the most thorough is *The Colorado Pass Book* by Don Koch (Pruett Publishing Company, 1982).

A Final Word

This book tells you where to find Colorado's highest passes and provides guidance for hiking to them. However, it doesn't tell you how to prepare for these trips. For those who want to reach these high passes, a substantial amount of hiking is required. If you are not an accomplished mountain hiker, you should refer to some of the excellent books covering such topics as equipment, getting in good physical condition, finding your way, hiking and climbing techniques, weather, and first aid.

I take the responsibility of describing these hikes to the best of my ability. These descriptions are based on the way things were at the time we hiked to these passes, updated by all of the more recent information that we have been able to obtain. You must take the responsibility of using good judgment when you take these hikes. Select hikes within your ability, have all of your equipment in good shape, and turn back in unfavorable weather.

Besides hiking to these passes with me, my wife Dotty has been a tireless helper in compiling the list of passes, writing the text, and typing the manuscript.

Others who have accompanied us on a hike to one or more of these passes are Mollie Graves, Ed Johnson, Carey Legett, Arthur and Kathy Lubinski, Bruce Martin, Jean Martin, Charley McCall, Gordon McKeague, Paul Pixler, and Art Tauchen. We have enjoyed their companionship on our trips to the high passes.

Hike Destinations

Destination

Passes	Elevation, Feet	Hike No.
Arapaho Pass	11,906	10
Argentine Pass	13,207	13
Avalanche Pass	12,100	33
Black Powder Pass	12,159	15
Blue Lake Pass	12,980	45
Boulder-Grand Pass	12,061	7
Browns Pass	12,020	24
Buckskin Pass	12,462	31
Caribou Pass	11,780	10
Chalk Creek Pass	12,140	27
Coffeepot Pass	12,740	38
Columbine Pass	12,700	48
Conundrum Pass	12,780	37
Cony Pass	12,420	8
Copper Pass	12,580	39
Denver Pass	12,900	43
Eccles Pass	11,900	16
Electric Pass	13,500	34
Elkhead Pass	13,220	23
Fall Creek Pass	12,580	20
Fancy Pass	12,380	21
French Pass	12,046	14
Frigid Air Pass	12,380	36
Granite Pass	12,100	4
Gunsight Pass	12,180	50
Gunsight Pass	12,167	26
Halfmoon Pass	12,520	42
Heckert Pass	12,700	29
Hunchback Pass	12,493	47
Keyhole, The	13,140	5
Kokomo Pass	12,022	19
Lake Pass	12,220	22
Napoleon Pass	12,020	25
Pawnee Pass	12,541	9
Ptarmigan Pass	12,180	3
Ptarmigan Pass	11,777	12
Richmond Pass	12,657	46

Destination

Passes	Elevation, Feet	Hike No.
Saddle, The	12,398	1
Searle Pass	12,020	18
Stone Man Pass	12,500	6
Storm Pass	12,460	41
Sunnyside Saddle	12,780	44
Timberline Pass	11,484	2
Trail Rider Pass	12,420	32
Triangle Pass	12,900	40
Trimble Pass	12,860	49
Uneva Pass	11,900	17
Vasquez Pass	11,700	11
Venable Pass	12,780	28
West Maroon Pass	12,500	35
Willow Pass	12,580	30

Lakes

Black Lake	10,620	6
Bluebird Lake	10,978	8
Cathedral Lake	11,866	34
Chickadee Pond	10,020	8
Copper Lake	11,321	39,40
Crater Lake	10,076	30,31
Crystal Lake	11,500	1
Dorothy, Lake	12,061	10
Eldorado Lake	12,504	47
Fancy Lake	11,540	21
Frozen Lake	11,580	6
Geneva Lake	10,936	32
Hancock Lake	11,660	27
Hunky Dory Lake	11,300	20
Isabelle, Lake	10,868	9
Jewel Lake	9,940	6
Junco Lake	11,620	8
Kite Lake	12,100	47
Lamphier Lake	11,700	26
Lawn Lake	10.987	1
Little Crystal Lake	11,500	1
Long Lake	10,521	9
Lost Lake	11,580	17

Lakes	Elevation, Feet	Hike No.
Many Winds, Lake of	11,620	7
Mills Lake	9,940	6
Ouzel Lake	10,020	8
Seven Sisters Lakes	12,000	20
Silver Dollar Pond	10,240	37,38
Snowmass Lake	10,980	29
Thunder Lake	10,574	7
Upper Hancock Lake	11,740	27
Wheeler Lakes	11,060	17

Other

	Elevation, Feet	Hike No.
Alberta Falls	9,400	4,6
Calypso Cascades	9,200	7,8
Conejos Falls	10,680	50
Conundrum Hot Springs	11,180	37,38
Copeland Falls	8,500	7,8
Flattop Mountain	12,324	3
Fourth of July Mine	11,260	10
Holy Cross City	11,408	20,21
Hunchback Mountain	13,136	47
Judd Falls	9,760	39,40
Ouzel Falls	9,400	7,8
Phantom Terrace	12,700	28
Three Forks	10,260	50
Tombstone Ridge	11,722	2

Trailhead Data

Hike No.	Trailhead	Elevation, Feet	Nearest Campground, Miles	Nearest Town, Miles	Miles Unpaved	Miles Less By 4WD
1	Horseshoe Park	8,550	Aspenglen-3	Estes Park-8	none	none
2	Trail Ridge Road	11,420	Aspenglen-12	Estes Park-17	none	none
3	Bear Lake	9,475	Glacier Basin-4	Estes Park-15	none	none
4	Glacier Gorge Junction	9,240	Glacier Basin-3	Estes Park-14	none	none
5	Longs Peak Ranger Station	9,383	Longs Peak-¼	Estes Park-12	1	none
6	Glacier Gorge Junction	9,240	Glacier Basin-3	Estes Park-14	none	none
7	Wild Basin Ranger Station	8,500	Copeland Lake-1½	Estes Park-18	1½	none
8	Wild Basin Ranger Station	8,500	Copeland Lake-1½	Estes Park-18	1½	none
9	Brainard Lake	10,500	Pawnee-1	Boulder-35	none	none
10	Buckingham Campground	10,100	Buckingham-0	Boulder-23	5	none
11	Jones Pass road	10,140	Mizraw-2½	Empire-8½	none	none
12	Silverthorne	9,140	—	Silverthorne-0	1	none
13	Peru Creek road	11,097	—	Dillon-16	9	none
14	Georgia Pass road	10,500	Michigan Creek-2¼	Fairplay-20	8½	none
15	Boreas Pass	11,481	Selkirk-4	Breckenridge-10	10	none
16	Interstate 70 near Frisco	9,140	Heaton Bay-2½	Frisco-2	½	none
17	Interstate 70 and Colorado 91	9,700	Black Lake-7	Frisco-7	none	none
18	Searle Gulch	11,100	—	Frisco-15	3½	none
19	East Fork Eagle River road	9,580	Tennessee Pass-7	Leadville-17	3½	none
20	off Homestake Reservoir road	10,280	Gold Park-5	Minturn-21½	11½	3
21	off Homestake Reservoir road	10,100	Gold Park-3½	Minturn-20	10	none
22	Pieplant road	10,260	Dinner Station-5	Gunnison-45	15	none

Hike No.	Trailhead	Elevation, Feet	Nearest Campground, Miles	Nearest Town, Miles	Miles Unpaved	Miles Less By 4WD
23	Vicksburg	9,660	—	Buena Vista-23	8	none
24	Cottonwood Pass road	9,900	Collegiate Peaks-1	Buena Vista-12	none	none
25	Cumberland Pass road	10,695	Quartz-4	Gunnison-36	7	3
26	Gold Creek Campground	10,030	Gold Creek-0	Gunnison-29	7	none
27	Hancock	11,040	Cascade-11	Buena Vista-28	12	3½
28	North Crestone Creek	8,800	North Crestone Creek-½	Alamosa-50	3	none
29	Snowmass Creek	8,420	Snowmass Creek-1	Basalt-14	5	none
30	Maroon Lake parking area	9,580	Maroon Lake-¼	Aspen-10	none	none
31	Maroon Lake parking area	9,580	Maroon Lake-¼	Aspen-10	none	none
32	near Crystal	9,000	Bogan Flats-11	Carbondale-34	5½	3
33	Lost Trail Creek road	9,060	Bogan Flats-8	Carbondale-31	2½	none
34	Ashcroft road	9,880	—	Aspen-13	½	none
35	Schofield Park	10,400	Gothic-5	Crested Butte-15	11	2
36	Schofield Park	10,400	Gothic-5	Crested Butte-15	11	2
37	Ashcroft road	8,760	—	Aspen-7	1	none
38	Ashcroft road	8,760	—	Aspen-7	1	none
39	Gothic	9,450	Avery Peak-1½	Crested Butte-8	4	none
40	Gothic	9,450	Avery Peak-1½	Crested Butte-8	4	none
41	Mill Creek road	9,000	—	Gunnison-17	4½	none
42	south of Stone Cellar Campground	10,180	Stone Cellar-7	Gunnison-58	27	2
43	Animas Forks	11,140	—	Silverton-13	11	4
44	Eureka Gulch	10,980	—	Silverton-11½	9½	4
45	Sneffels Creek	10,780	Amphitheatre-8	Ouray-8	7½	4
46	US 550 south of Ouray	9,900	Amphitheatre-7½	Ouray-8½	none	none
47	Cunningham Creek road	10,460	—	Silverton-9	7	none
48	Needleton	8,212	—	Silverton	none	none
49	Needleton	8,212	—	Silverton	none	none
50	Platoro Reservoir road	10,140	Mix Lake-7½	Platoro-8	35	none

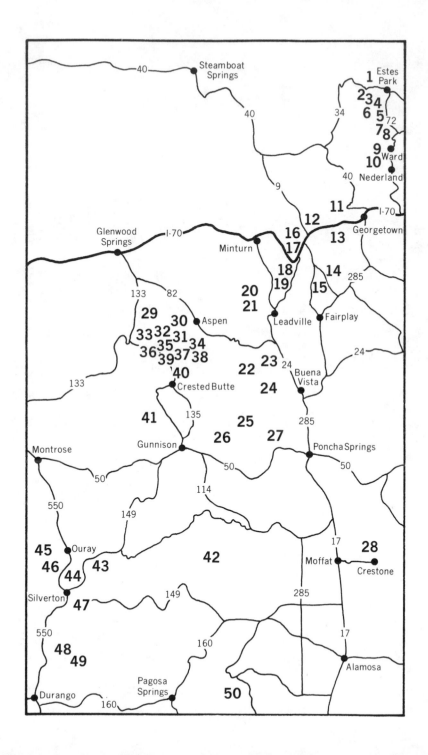

The Hikes

1. The Saddle

Elevation: 12,398 feet
Hiking distance: 16 miles
Starting elevation: 8,550 feet
Elevation gain: 3,900 feet
Rating: moderate, good trail but long
Estimated time: 10 hours

Maps:
7.5 minute Estes Park
(trailhead area and a short section of trail only)
7.5 minute Trail Ridge
Rocky Mountain National Park

The pass called "The Saddle" is in the Mummy Range, situated in the northern part of Rocky Mountain National Park. It is the most northerly of the Colorado passes above twelve thousand feet. The Saddle is the low point on the ridge between Hagues Peak and Fairchild Mountain. Going to The Saddle makes a fine hike, long enough to require a full day of hiking.

Drive on Trail Ridge Road about two miles west of the Fall River entrance to Rocky Mountain National Park. There is a parking area at the trailhead for hikes to Lawn Lake and Ypsilon Lake. Begin the hike by following the popular scenic trail to Lawn Lake. After a mile, take the right fork where a trail to the left goes to Ypsilon Lake.

Along the trail toward Lawn Lake and The Saddle.

A view of The Saddle from the trail below Lawn Lake. *Photo by Gordon McKeague.*

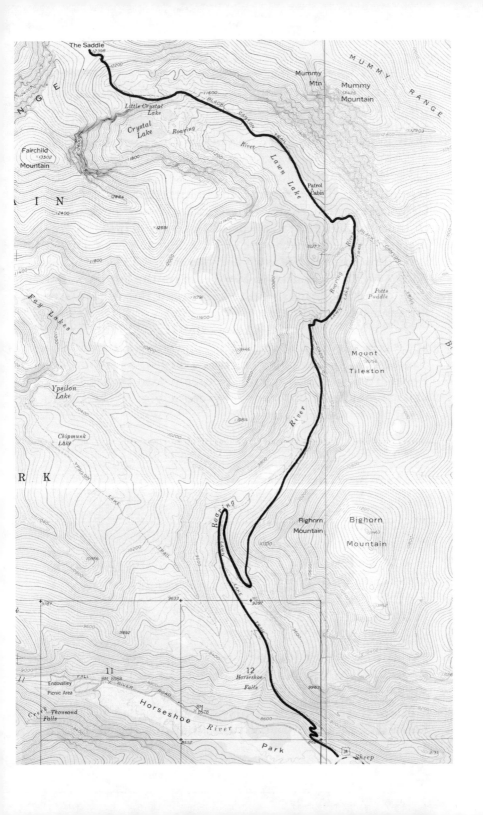

Four more miles of steady climbing on the east side of the Roaring River brings you to another trail junction. The Black Canyon trail goes to the right and passes Potts Puddle. Our route takes the left fork at this junction. In less than a mile you reach Lawn Lake, which is near timberline.

Continue on the trail along the northeast side of Lawn Lake. A half mile beyond the lake, take the right fork at a trail junction. The left fork leads to Little Crystal Lake and Crystal Lake. The route to The Saddle follows the drainage to the west as the trail becomes less well defined. A trail really isn't needed in this area, as the objective is obvious. It is the low point to the west between rugged Hagues Peak on the right and Fairchild Mountain on the left. Another mile of hiking brings you to the broad flat tundra area known as The Saddle.

Unlike trails to most passes, the trail to The Saddle approaches from just one side. The view west from The Saddle is into the valley of Hague Creek, a stream that flows from south to north. A descent into Hague Creek valley would be quite steep. Therefore, you will be glad to return the way you came.

2. Timberline Pass

Elevation: 11,484 feet
Hiking distance: 4 miles
Starting elevation: 11,420 feet
Elevation gain: 650 feet
Rating: easy
Estimated time: 3 hours

Maps:
7.5 minute Trail Ridge
Rocky Mountain National Park

In contrast to the long hikes to other high passes of Rocky Mountain National Park, the hike to Timberline

Looking back at Trail Ridge Road and the trailhead for the hike to Timberline Pass.

Pass is short. The hike follows a section of the Ute Trail, an old Indian route, and it doesn't involve a lot of elevation gain. This hike makes a good choice for those not wanting to try the long hikes to the higher passes. Surprisingly, for such a short hike in a scenic area, there aren't likely to be many other hikers on the trail.

The trailhead is about three quarters of a mile east of Forest Canyon Overlook on Trail Ridge Road at a point known as Ute Crossing. Driving from the east, the starting point is about two miles west of Rainbow Curve. The trailhead, at 11,420 feet, is almost as high as Timberline Pass. The trail starts on the south side of the road just opposite an old road that once led to three stone cabins. These cabins have been removed, and the area is being restored to its natural state.

The walk to Timberline Pass takes you along Tombstone Ridge, a scenic area of weird rock formations that extends southeast from Trail Ridge Road. The route follows the old Ute Trail, which is marked by small cairns that help you find the way when the trail is indistinct. From the trailhead, the trail climbs about two hundred feet to a level

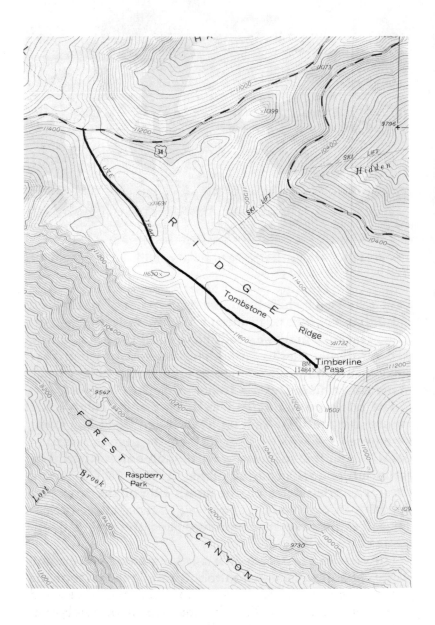

Rocky points along Tombstone Ridge.

area. After crossing the level area, there is a short descent and then another climb to the high point of the hike at 11,660 feet. From this elevation on Tombstone Ridge, the trail descends gradually to Timberline Pass.

Unlike most passes, Timberline Pass is so obscure that it may be hard to find. The pass is south of the high point on Tombstone Ridge, but it is not framed by a similar high point on the other side. The highest point on the ridge south of Timberline Pass is no more than thirty feet higher than the pass.

The Ute Trail descends steeply and enters the timber after crossing Timberline Pass. It continues on down Windy Gulch into Beaver Meadows. With proper transportation arrangements, a one-way downhill hike can be made. Otherwise, the route is back along Tombstone Ridge.

On the return, pay particular attention to the impressive views of Forest Canyon to the south and west. As you face Forest Canyon, the northwest flanks of Stones Peak are on your left, and Terra Tomah Mountain is on your right. These mountains frame Hayden Gorge, which runs southwest from Forest Canyon.

3. Ptarmigan Pass

Elevation: 12,180 feet
Hiking distance: 10 miles
Starting elevation: 9,475 feet
Elevation gain: 2,800 feet
Rating: easy
Estimated time: 8 hours

Maps:
7.5 minute McHenrys Peak
Rocky Mountain National Park

A long, scenic trek across the Continental Divide in Rocky Mountain National Park will take you to Ptarmigan Pass. It is a unique pass in that you come down to it rather than climb up to reach it. When you're walking along the divide on the broad, flat tundra, it's hard to tell exactly when you've reached Ptarmigan Pass.

A strenuous one-way hike from one side of the Continental Divide to the other, crossing Ptarmigan Pass, is well worth the effort. However, Ptarmigan Pass can be visited on a shorter out-and-back hike. The information in the heading is based on an out-and-back hike.

The trailhead is at Bear Lake, the popular tourist area in the heart of Rocky Mountain National Park. From the parking area, hike north along the east side of Bear Lake to get on the well-used trail to Flattop Mountain. This excellent trail ascends 2,800 feet in about four and a half miles. In the first mile there are two trail junctions. After a half mile, take the left fork where the right fork goes to Bierstadt Lake. A half mile farther, again take the left fork where another right fork leads to Fern Lake and Odessa Lake.

Continue on the Flattop Mountain trail to a trail junction marked by giant cairns on the western part of the broad summit of Flattop Mountain. From this trail junction, two trails continue down to the Colorado River valley on the

Hallett Peak on the left and Flattop Mountain. The trail to Ptarmigan Pass ascends the long ridge of Flattop Mountain from right to left.

western side of the park. The left fork leads down the North Inlet to reach the valley near Grand Lake. The right fork follows Tonahutu Creek to the highway north of Grand Lake. The Tonahutu Creek trail is the one that leads over Ptarmigan Pass.

At the trail junction on Flattop Mountain, take the right fork—the Tonahutu Creek trail—which descends somewhat as it heads west. Within a quarter of a mile, it meets a spur trail leading in from the left. After passing the junction with the spur trail, less than a half mile of gradual descent brings you to Ptarmigan Pass.

Ptarmigan Pass, at an elevation of 12,180 feet, is on the Continental Divide at the low point between Flattop Mountain and Ptarmigan Point. Ptarmigan Point is the knobby summit to the north. Ptarmigan Pass is a Continental Divide crossing between the Fern Creek valley on the east and the Ptarmigan Creek drainage on the west. However, there is no defined route across the pass between these two drainages.

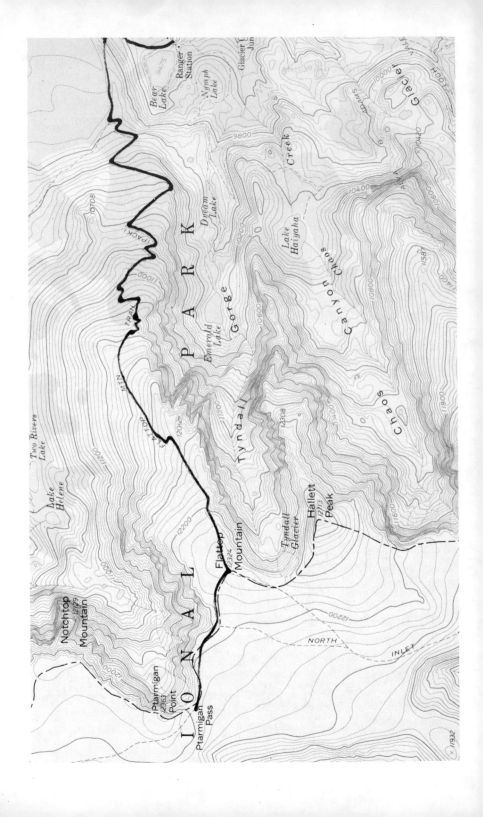

A pause along the trail to Ptarmigan Pass.

Once you've reached Ptarmigan Pass, if transportation arrangements have been made, you can continue on trail for eleven more miles to the highway. The route takes you around the western side of Ptarmigan Point to Bighorn Flats, a vast, flat area near the Continental Divide. The trail crosses Bighorn Flats and descends along Tonahutu Creek. About nine miles from Ptarmigan Pass, the trail rounds a large, flat area known as Big Meadows. On the western side of Big Meadows you come to a trail junction. Although

A look down into the gorge east of Ptarmigan Pass. *Photo by Gordon McKeague.*

both trails from this junction eventually lead to the highway, the shortest route is to turn right and follow the Green Mountain trail.

If you aren't making the long one-way hike, it's a five-mile walk back over Flattop Mountain and down the trail from Ptarmigan Pass to Bear Lake.

4. Granite Pass

Elevation: 12,100 feet
Hiking distance: 16 miles
Starting elevation: 9,240 feet
Elevation gain: 2,800 feet
Rating: easy, but fairly long
Estimated time: 9 hours

Maps:
7.5 minute Longs Peak
7.5 minute McHenrys Peak
Rocky Mountain National Park

Granite Pass makes a good objective for those who want to hike a Longs Peak trail and don't want to go all the way to the peak. On the other hand, many climbers of Longs Peak walk right by Granite Pass without realizing that they have come to one of Colorado's highest passes.

The most popular trailhead for a hike to Longs Peak is at Longs Peak Ranger Station on the east side of Rocky Mountain National Park. However, for the hike to Granite Pass, we prefer the approach from the north, which is described after a review of the popular eastern route.

To approach from the east, leave Colorado 7 south of Estes Park and drive west on a spur road toward Longs Peak Campground. The ranger station is at the large parking area just beyond the campground entrance. For a

Bridge across Glacier Creek on the trail to Granite Pass.

Granite Pass. *Photo by Gordon McKeague.*

Trail junction—the left fork leads to Granite Pass while the right fork leads to Stone Man Pass.

summer weekend, the best hiking instructions would be to start at the trailhead and follow the crowd.

After a mile, take the left fork where the trail to the right goes to Eugenia Mine. Three more miles on the well-traveled trail bring you to another trail junction. The trail to the left ascends Mills Moraine and rounds the northeast flank of Mount Lady Washington. Many hikers choose the right fork through Jims Grove. This is a steeper but more direct route that goes directly west from the junction.

The two routes converge about a quarter mile below Granite Pass. Continue northwest from this point to another trail junction within a quarter of a mile. From this second trail junction, the trail to Longs Peak goes left and climbs on switchbacks southwest to Boulder Field on the west side of Mount Lady Washington. The right-fork trail brings you to Granite Pass in about a hundred yards. Those who have hiked the Longs Peak trail without walking this short stretch have not been to Granite Pass.

While the most popular route to Granite Pass is via the eastern approach, we suggest a hike to Granite Pass from the north. The northern approach is longer, but it has several advantages. Because it is not generally used as an approach to Longs Peak, there will be few other hikers on the northern trail compared with the hordes on the trail from the east. Approaching from the north, Granite Pass can be the principal objective, and by stopping there you won't appear to be a dropout among Longs Peak climbers.

The trailhead for this northern approach is at Glacier Gorge Junction, on the Bear Lake road in Rocky Mountain National Park. Hike southeast on the popular trail to pass Alberta Falls in a half mile. Three-fourths of a mile of gradual climbing beyond Alberta Falls brings you to a trail junction. Here the route to The Loch, Sky Pond, Mills Lake, Black Lake, and other assorted objectives bears right around the south side of Glacier Knobs. The route to Granite Pass stays left and goes downhill to cross Glacier Creek.

Once down and across Glacier Creek, the trail climbs gradually to the east and then bears south. After climbing to about 10,300 feet through the mostly open country, a trail junction is reached. The left fork is the trail coming up along Boulder Brook. Keep right to ascend on switchbacks to the broad tundra area northwest of Battle Mountain. Gradual climbing on the trail across this seemingly endless area brings you to Granite Pass.

At Granite Pass, Mount Lady Washington is to the south, and Battle Mountain is to the northeast. Battle Mountain, off the flank of Mount Lady Washington, consists of a series of ridge points but has no well-defined summit. The ridge point that is 12,044 feet high is considered to be the summit of Battle Mountain. Granite Pass is up the ridge southwest of Battle Mountain toward Mount Lady Washington and actually is slightly higher than the summit of Battle Mountain.

If you can make suitable transportation arrangements, an attractive one-way hike can be made between Glacier Gorge Junction and the Longs Peak Ranger Station, with Granite Pass as the high point.

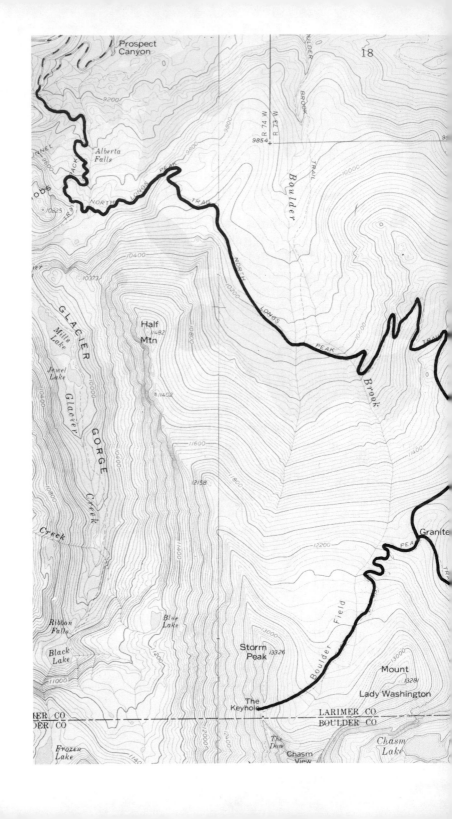

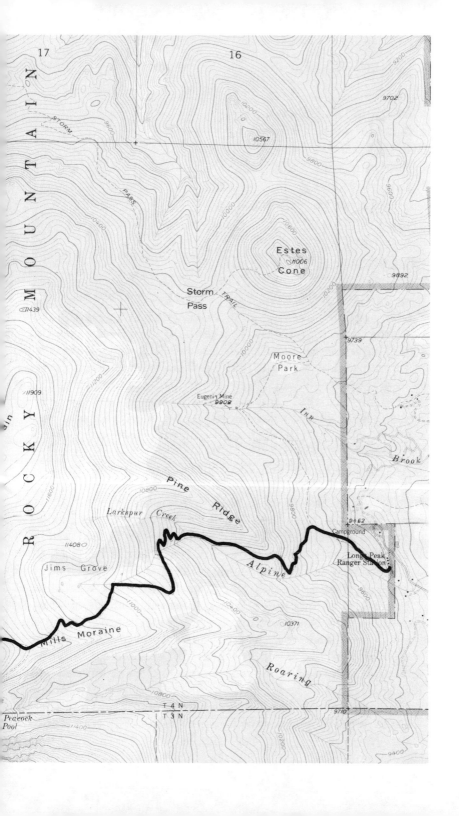

5. The Keyhole

Elevation: 13,140 feet
Hiking distance: 15 miles
Starting elevation: 9,380 feet
Elevation gain: 3,900 feet
Rating: moderate
Estimated time: 9 hours

Maps:
7.5 minute Longs Peak
Rocky Mountain National Park

Many people have walked through The Keyhole without realizing that it is a pass. It is one of the few Colorado passes without the word "pass," "saddle," "gap," or "divide" in its name. The Keyhole is the low point between Longs Peak and Storm Peak. It is one of only four Colorado passes above thirteen thousand feet that are on hiking routes. Since it is on the popular hiking trail to Longs Peak, The Keyhole may have had more foot traffic than any other Colorado high pass.

To reach The Keyhole, follow one of the routes described for a hike to Granite Pass in the preceding section. From the trail junction just southeast of Granite Pass, continue southwest on the trail toward Longs Peak. Climb on switchbacks on the west side of Mount Lady Washington into the large basin north of Longs Peak. This basin, known as Boulder Field, is flanked by Mount Lady Washington on the east and Storm Peak on the west.

After you enter Boulder Field, the unique shape of The Keyhole at the low point on the ridge northwest of Longs Peak comes into view. Make your way across the giant rocks of Boulder Field toward The Keyhole. As you approach, notice a shelter cabin below and to the left of The Keyhole.

When you reach The Keyhole, you can look down to the west into the upper part of Glacier Gorge. The trail from

The Keyhole. *Photo by Art Tauchen.*

View west from The Keyhole toward Chiefs Head Peak. *Photo by Gordon McKeague.*

The Keyhole to Longs Peak descends only slightly before contouring and climbing along the west flank of the peak. If your destination is The Keyhole, return back across Boulder Field.

The Keyhole could be approached from the western side, but with much greater effort. The difficult western approach involves a hard trail hike to Black Lake, a walk up the gorge toward Green Lake, and then a stiff, rocky climb of about 2,500 feet to The Keyhole.

The data at the beginning of this hike description is based on starting the hike at Longs Peak Ranger Station. If you start at Glacier Gorge Junction, the round-trip distance is about four miles greater, and the elevation gain is slightly more than starting at Longs Peak Ranger Station. The eastern approach from Longs Peak Ranger Station is the shorter and the easier if you wish to reach both Granite Pass and The Keyhole on the same hike.

6. Stone Man Pass

Elevation: 12,500 feet
Hiking distance: 14 miles
Starting elevation: 9,240 feet
Elevation gain: 3,500 feet
Rating: difficult
Estimated time: 11 hours

Maps:
7.5 minute McHenrys Peak
Rocky Mountain National Park

Stone Man Pass lies on the Continental Divide in the central part of Rocky Mountain National Park. It gets its name from the distinctive rock formation that stands next to the pass. Stone Man Pass is the low point on the ridge between Chiefs Head Peak and McHenrys Peak.

Stone Man Pass in the distance. Chiefs Head Peak is left and McHenrys Peak is right of the pass.

McHenrys Peak is generally considered the hardest mountain to climb of the peaks higher than thirteen thousand feet in Rocky Mountain National Park. Getting to Stone Man Pass on the route to McHenrys Peak is the hardest part of climbing McHenrys Peak. Consequently, Stone Man Pass is one of the hardest climbs of the Colorado passes above twelve thousand feet. Be prepared for a long day.

The trailhead is at Glacier Gorge Junction, the starting point for hikes to The Loch, Sky Pond, Mills Lake, and Black Lake, as well as the northern route to Longs Peak. For the hike to Stone Man Pass, follow the trail to Black Lake. This five-mile hike is a challenge in itself, since the latter part of the trail is slow going with many turns, twists, ups, and downs. After a half mile, you pass Alberta Falls, and in another three-fourths of a mile you reach the trail junction with the northern trail to Longs Peak. Take the right fork at this junction and go three-fourths of a mile farther to another trail junction. The left fork here leads past Mills Lake and Jewel Lake on its way to Black Lake.

Glacier Gorge from above Black Lake. *Photo by Gordon McKeague.*

Stone Man Pass is southwest of Black Lake. Once at Black Lake, it first is necessary to circle the lake and climb to the bench beyond. The lake can be circled on either side, but the easiest though slightly longer route is to round the lake on the left. Start up a route along the drainage leading in from the east. This would be the route to follow if you were going to Blue Lake or Green Lake.

After following this drainage to get beyond the steeper cliffs, turn sharply right and go generally southwest. Following the line of least resistance through the rock slabs and tundra, continue to make your way west and southwest. The "Stone Man" rock formation to the left of Stone Man Pass should be clearly visible. Cross the outlet from Frozen Lake, and head for the base of a steep gully just below the pass. Here the slopes become much steeper. Now it's a climb of only about three hundred feet to the pass.

Extreme care should be exercised for the rest of the climb. If the steep gully is filled with snow, only those with experience and proper equipment for climbing steep snowfields should attempt the climb. If the route is up the rocky gully free of snow, look for the most solid stepping stones. Because of the danger of dislodging rocks, it's best for climbers to stay side-by-side rather than be one above the other. Once you have ascended this short, steep gully, you will be at Stone Man Pass.

If you also want to climb McHenrys Peak on this trip, it's another nine hundred feet of rocky climbing along and to the left of the ridge leading northwest to the peak. It's also possible to climb Chiefs Head Peak from Stone Man Pass by following the ridge to the southeast. However, there are easier ways of getting to Chiefs Head Peak.

Return from Stone Man Pass the way you came, being as careful going down the rock gully as you were coming up.

7. Boulder-Grand Pass

Elevation: 12,061 feet
Hiking distance: 17 miles
Starting elevation: 8,500 feet
Elevation gain: 3,800 feet
Rating: difficult
Estimated time: 11 hours

Maps:
7.5 minute Allens Park
7.5 minute Isolation Peak
Rocky Mountain National Park

A long trail walk to a large scenic lake, an off-trail venture to a remote higher lake, and a stiff climb will bring you to Boulder-Grand Pass. The trip is well worth the effort, even though it is a long hike with lots of elevation gain. Because of the long hike and steep climb, Boulder-Grand Pass is one of the more difficult to reach of the Colorado passes above twelve thousand feet.

Thunder Lake and
Boulder-Grand
Pass.
*Photo by
Gordon McKeague.*

Start with the popular all-day tourist hike to Thunder
Lake. The trailhead for this hike is at Wild Basin Ranger
Station in the southern part of Rocky Mountain National
Park. The entry point is south of Estes Park off Colorado 7,
between Meeker Park and Allens Park. The narrow two-
mile road leads west to a small parking area near the ranger
station.

The walk to Thunder Lake is on excellent, well-used
trail. This trail gains twenty-four hundred feet of elevation
over the seven-mile route. The trail first passes Copeland
Falls in less than a half mile. Continuing through the
forest, the trail reaches the junction of North St. Vrain
Creek and Cony Creek. It continues along Cony Creek to
soon reach Calypso Cascades, a tumble of water coming
down Cony Creek from the south. Take the right-hand

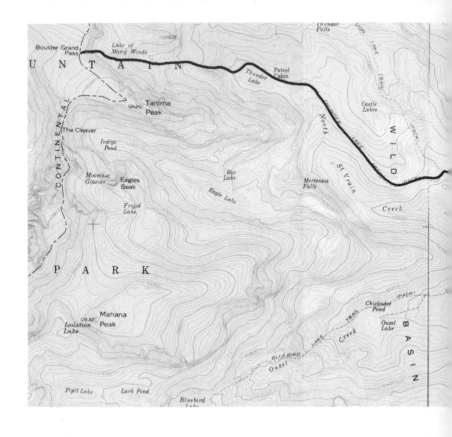

trail at Calypso Cascades, and climb gradually to Ouzel
Falls and soon thereafter to another trail junction. Here,
take the right fork to Thunder Lake. The left fork is the
trail to Bluebird Lake. Scenery along the way and the views
from the eastern side of Thunder Lake make this a popular
hike.

After you reach Thunder Lake, the harder climbing
begins. You can look across the lake to the west and pick
out the route toward Boulder-Grand Pass. Mount Alice is
to the right of the pass, and Tanima Peak is to the left. Go
around the northern shore of Thunder Lake, and cross two
drainages coming into Thunder Lake from the west. The

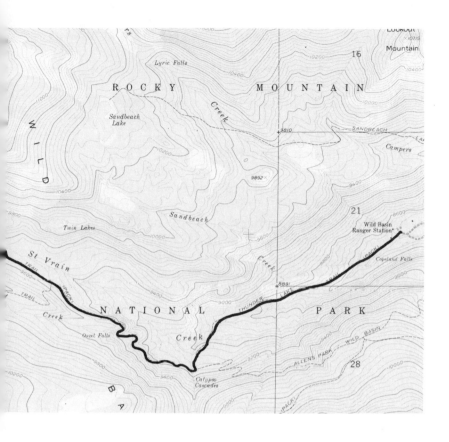

first drainage comes down from Falcon Lake and the second drainage from Lake of Many Winds, your next objective. Continue to follow the second drainage westward. A mile of climbing through the timber, tundra, and rocks brings you to Lake of Many Winds, much smaller than Thunder Lake.

Climb left of Lake of Many Winds, and continue on west toward Boulder-Grand Pass. The climbing gets steeper when you get beyond the lake. For more secure footing, it is best to climb on the more stable rocky outcrops on either side of the steep rocky drainage. Through this stretch of climbing, there is some danger of falling rocks. However, the distance is short, and the grade gets more gradual as you near the pass.

It takes only about three hundred feet of climbing on the steep rocky stretch to bring you to Boulder-Grand Pass. The broad area of tundra at the pass extends almost a half mile to the west, after which the terrain drops off sharply.

The route to Boulder-Grand Pass from the west is even longer than the one through Wild Basin. It starts with a long hike up the East Inlet on the trail to Lake Verna. Then there's a stretch to some higher lakes and a stiff climb to the Continental Divide. One of the routes for climbing Mount Alice, on the Continental Divide north of the pass, is via Boulder-Grand Pass. Mount Alice is only a little over a mile north of the pass, but is almost thirteen hundred feet higher. Tanima Peak, to the southeast, also is approached from Boulder-Grand Pass. It is a half-mile walk from the pass along the Continental Divide on gradual slopes to the Tanima Peak summit.

Return from Boulder-Grand Pass by the same route you came.

A look back from Boulder-Grand Pass. Lake of Many Winds is in the foreground and Thunder Lake is in the distance.

8. Cony Pass

Elevation: 12,420 feet
Hiking distance: 19 miles
Starting elevation: 8,500 feet
Elevation gain: 4,500 feet
Rating: difficult
Estimated time: 13 hours

Maps:
7.5 minute Allens Park
7.5 minute Isolation Peak
Rocky Mountain National Park

Cony Pass is just east of the Continental Divide in the southern part of Rocky Mountain National Park. It is the low point on the ridge that runs eastward from the divide to Mount Copeland. The hike to Cony Pass is one of the more difficult of the hikes to Colorado high passes. The trek requires a long walk on trail followed by some tough off-trail climbing with a final steep ascent to the pass.

The starting point is at the Wild Basin Ranger Station, two miles west of Colorado 9 in the southern part of Rocky Mountain National Park. This is the same trailhead as for Boulder-Grand Pass. The shortest route to Cony Pass starts by taking the seven-mile trail to Bluebird Lake, a good day's hike in itself. On the route to Bluebird Lake, a trail junction is reached about a mile beyond Calypso Cascades. The trail to the right goes to Thunder Lake. You take the trail to the left. The trail ascends a ridge and proceeds more than a mile without much elevation gain through a depressing area burned over in recent years. You soon pass a side trail to the left which goes to Ouzel Lake. Another mile through burned timber and a mile of rather rugged, rocky trail-climbing finally brings you to Bluebird Lake.

From the dam at Bluebird Lake, walk along the shore to the south on the left side of the lake. Ascend the rocky

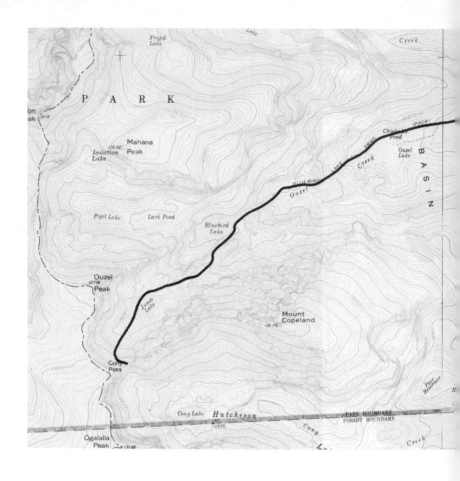

ridge south of the lake. This ridge is between Bluebird Lake
and the outlet from Junco Lake. A good route starts out
along a ramp that leads southwest and bypasses the first
large rock formation along the ridge. After reaching a
saddle at 11,260 feet, beyond the first rocky ridge point,
ascend southwest to the top of the ridge. You can ascend
either directly up a narrow gully or up a grassy ramp on the
left along the south side of the ridge. Once on top of the
ridge, climb up its grassy slopes and walk along large, flat
rocks to reach Junco Lake at 11,620 feet.

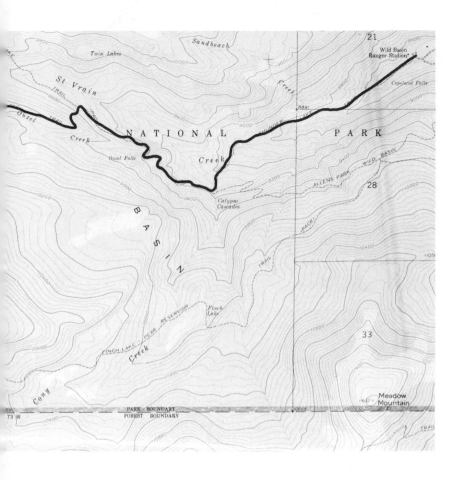

From Junco Lake, Cony Pass can be seen as the low point to the south. Cony Pass is flanked on the left by the ragged ridge from Mount Copeland. To the right of Cony Pass, a steep cliff extends up to the Continental Divide. The divide runs smoothly from these cliffs toward Ouzel Peak on the right.

Walk around the right side of Junco Lake, staying as near to the lake as possible. From the southwestern end of Junco Lake, pick out the best route to Cony Pass. This will depend on snow conditions and your personal preferences.

Burned area on the trail to Cony Pass.

Bluebird Lake from the ridge route to Junco Lake.

Junco Lake and Cony Pass.

The eight-hundred-foot climb from Junco Lake to Cony Pass is steep and tiresome at best. If the snows have receded, a grassy route to the right of the pass can take you high up the steep slopes and avoid some of the loose rocks. From high on the grassy slope, a climb to the left above some rocky buttresses brings you to a more level contour and to the pass. Some climbers may prefer the shorter, steep, rocky route directly from the lake to the pass. When following this route, care is required to avoid rockfall danger.

At Cony Pass, the view south is toward rugged Elk Tooth on the left and the flank of higher and flatter Ogalalla Peak on the right. Cony Lake is down the steep slopes in the basin below. The rounded, grassy summit of St. Vrain Mountain may be seen further away and left of Elk Tooth.

The view back over Junco Lake reveals a grandiose scene with Longs Peak and Mount Meeker directly north of the valley.

There is no evidence of a trail or road over Cony Pass from either side. The fact that the two valleys on either

Cony Lake and Elk Tooth from Cony Pass.

side of Cony Pass join east of Mount Copeland should
mean that there never was any need for substantial traffic
over Cony Pass.

Return the way you came. It may be easier to descend a
rocky route directly to Junco Lake. In descending the ridge
from Junco Lake to Bluebird Lake, pay close attention to
finding an easy route off the ridge down to Bluebird Lake.

9. Pawnee Pass

Elevation: 12,541 feet
Hiking distance: 9 miles
Starting elevation: 10,500 feet
Elevation gain: 2,200 feet
Rating: easy
Estimated time: 5 hours

Maps:
7.5 minute Ward
7.5 minute Monarch Lake
Roosevelt National Forest

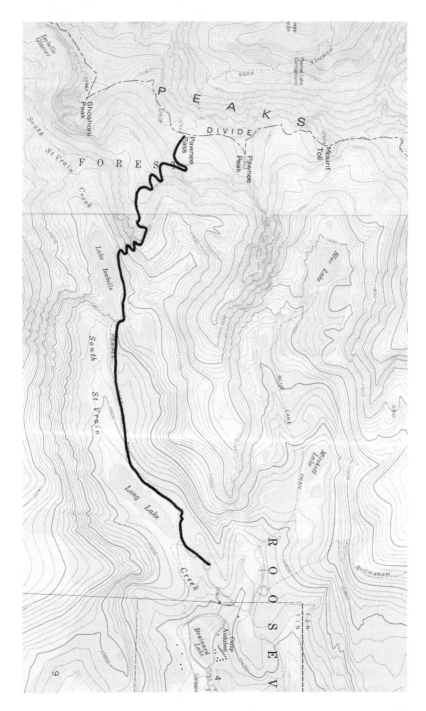

Pawnee Pass is reached by good trail in a popular hiking area—the Indian Peaks Wilderness south of Rocky Mountain National Park. The starting point is at Brainard Lake, a crowded tourist area in the summer.

From just north of Ward on Colorado 72, drive west on paved road to Brainard Lake. There are two trailheads on the west side of Brainard Lake, west of the road that circles the lake. The first trailhead that you reach as you drive around the north side of Brainard Lake is for hikes to Mitchell Lake and Blue Lake. Continue on to the next trailhead, which is for hikes to Long Lake and Lake Isabelle, as well as Pawnee Pass.

The excellent, well-traveled trail climbs gradually west and in less than a half mile passes along the dam at the east end of Long Lake. A left fork of the trail crosses the dam, but the trail to Pawnee Pass stays north of Long Lake and does not cross the dam. Another mile of hiking on the trail through the timber north of South St. Vrain Creek brings you to a creek crossing. Here the trail continues with steeper climbing to the north side of Lake Isabelle. After proceeding along the north shore of Lake Isabelle, the trail leaves the lake and climbs steadily to the north on switchbacks to gain the crest of a ridge. The trail follows this ridge west and then bears northwest through a rocky area on more switchbacks. The route levels out as it crosses the tundra to reach Pawnee Pass. The steepest part of the climb is from Lake Isabelle to the pass, with an elevation gain of eighteen hundred feet in this section.

Pawnee Pass is in a broad and almost flat area on the Continental Divide. A half mile north is Pawnee Peak, only four hundred feet higher. Shoshoni Peak is down the ridge to the south at about the same elevation as Pawnee Peak, but it is beyond two intermediate ridge points.

Pawnee Pass can also be approached from the west, starting at Monarch Lake. This route is longer and involves about two thousand feet more elevation gain, but it is likely to be far less crowded. A trail starts up Buchanan Creek and then turns up Cascade Creek. Higher up it reaches Pawnee Lake and then makes a steep climb on switchbacks to Pawnee Pass.

10. Arapaho Pass and Caribou Pass

Elevation: 11,906 feet and 11,780 feet
Hiking distance: 10 miles
Starting elevation: 10,100 feet
Elevation gain: 2,300 feet
Rating: easy
Estimated time: 6 hours

Maps:
7.5 minute East Portal
7.5 minute Monarch Lake
Roosevelt National Forest

This hike combines two passes in the Indian Peaks Wilderness with a spectacular trail between them. The first part of the hike is on a recently constructed trail that leads to an old mine. The middle portion of the hike follows an old mine trail that gradually climbs a rocky hillside to

Trail to Arapaho Pass.

Old equipment at the Fourth of July Mine. Arapaho Pass is in the distance.

Trail from Arapaho Pass to Caribou Pass.

Lake Dorothy.

Arapaho Pass. The views along the way make this a very pleasurable hike.

Drive on Colorado 72 or Colorado 119 to Nederland, which is west of Boulder. From the southern part of Nederland, take the paved road west through Eldora. About a mile west of Eldora, follow the right fork up the hill

Drive the solid but bumpy gravel road four miles to Buckingham Campground. The trailhead is at the parking area in the upper northwest portion of the campground area.

A trail built in 1981 leaves the parking area and climbs the hillside to the northwest. This excellent trail replaces a former route on an old road up the valley.

After a mile or so on the trail, which provides excellent views across the valley, a trail junction is reached. The trail to Diamond Lake continues straight ahead, while the trail that you should follow to Arapaho Pass switches back to the right. A climb through the forest and some clambering over rocks for another long mile bring you to the Fourth of July Mine. Just some old equipment and some filled-in mines remain here.

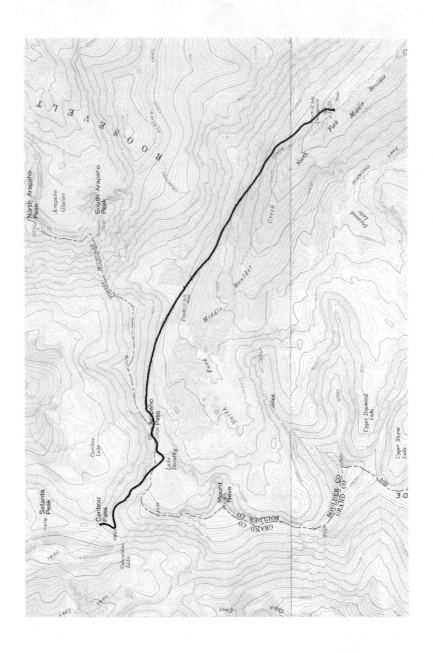

40

Caribou Lake from Caribou Pass.

At the mine, a trail heads uphill and back to the east toward the Arapaho Glacier. The trail to Arapaho Pass may be seen continuing ahead, gradually climbing to the pass. Hike a mile on this rocky but solidly built trail to reach Arapaho Pass.

The sensational view west from Arapaho Pass is toward Caribou Pass, with the slightly higher Satanta Peak to the right. Look sharply to see the trail to Caribou Pass carved into the cliffs to the left. The trail is there even though you may not be able to pick it out completely.

Although Caribou Pass is lower than Arapaho Pass, the trail first takes you higher. Follow the Continental Divide ridge west for a view of Lake Dorothy, set in a cirque surrounded by mountains on the divide. Mount Neva is the high point south of Lake Dorothy. The dramatic view back to the northeast is of North Arapaho Peak.

Continue on the trail past the views of Lake Dorothy to contour and descend along the northeast side of the steep cliffs extending toward Caribou Pass. Careful walking is required where slides have narrowed the trail. A wider tread brings you down the last stretch to Caribou Pass.

Looking back to Arapaho Pass from Caribou Pass, a switchback trail from Arapaho Pass down to Caribou Lake in the valley below can be plainly seen. Apache Peak and Navajo Peak are the striking high points to the northeast. Trails lead down to the west from both Arapaho and Caribou passes, but the return route is the way you came.

11. Vasquez Pass

Elevation: 11,700 feet
Hiking distance: 4 miles
Starting elevation: 10,140 feet
Elevation gain: 1,700 feet
Rating: moderate, short but steep
Estimated time: 4 hours

Maps:
7.5 minute Berthoud Pass
Arapaho National Forest

If you like to venture off the established trails, do a little route finding, and climb some steep slopes, this is a good hike for you. It is short enough to do in a half day, and the trailhead is near a major highway. The hike provides dramatic scenery for a route that goes only a little over a mile, as the crow flies, from a paved road. On the other hand, if you like to stick to established trails, this hike to Vasquez Pass is not for you.

The trailhead is off US 40 between Interstate 70 and Berthoud Pass. Drive to the west end of the long switchback that is about midway between these points. Turn west on paved road at this switchback and immediately come to Big Bend Picnic Ground. From the parking area at the picnic ground, drive exactly one mile west to find an obscure creek coming from the north and entering a culvert on the right-hand side of the road. This

Red Mountain south of the route to Vasquez Pass.

Approaching Vasquez Pass.

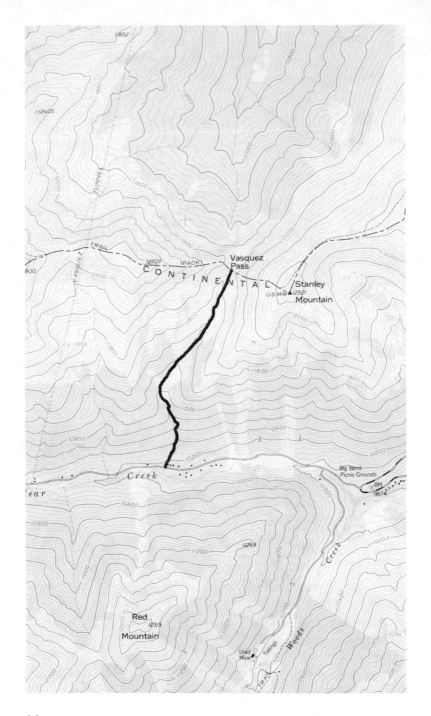

Looking south from Vasquez Pass.

creek is just beyond a large, flat area on the north side of
the road. Park here. We'll call this area the trailhead,
although there isn't any trail to be seen.

From the eastern end of the flat parking area, set out
uphill on the right-hand side of the creek. This creek,
which becomes more prominent as you move away from
the road, will be on your left all the way to Vasquez Pass.
Stay within hearing distance of the creek, but not so close
to it that you get in the deep gorge with its thick brush.

Hopefully, as you climb from the parking area, you will
run across an old switchbacking trail. This unmaintained
trail will take you up the steep slope a little easier than
climbing it directly. Higher up, you may run across
numerous game trails that make the climbing easier. The
creek bends first to the east and then back toward the west
as you climb the steep slope. Several waterfalls can be seen
along the way.

After climbing to about eleven thousand feet, the grade
slackens to make the climbing easier. In this area of sparse
timber, you get glimpses of the pass ahead. About four
hundred feet of additional climbing brings you to open

45

country. From here you can look back across the valley to Red Mountain, and you can see the Henderson Mine operations below. Some sketchy trails, in an area where they really aren't needed, take you the rest of the way to Vasquez Pass.

Vasquez Pass is on the Continental Divide and is crossed by an indicated trail along the divide. But that trail isn't any more noticeable than some of the ones you've come on. There is the indication of a trail starting down toward the valley north of the pass.

Recently signs have been posted prohibiting parking along the road west of Big Bend Picnic Ground. The large flat area mentioned in the second paragraph has been blocked off. If parking is restricted when you are there, it is best to park at the picnic ground and walk a mile west up the road before following the creek north.

12. Ptarmigan Pass

Elevation: 11,777 feet
Hiking distance: 16 miles
Starting elevation: 9,140 feet
Elevation gain: 3,500 feet
Rating: moderate; easy walking but long
Estimated time: 8 hours

Maps:
7.5 minute Dillon
Arapaho National Forest

The hike to Ptarmigan Pass is long and scenic. Most of the route is on good trail, but as you approach the pass, the trail becomes obscure. One unusual feature of this hike is that you first cross a slightly higher unnamed pass. Then you descend into another valley before climbing to Ptarmigan Pass.

Ptarmigan Pass is a crossing of the main ridge of the

Start of the route to Ptarmigan Pass.

Williams Fork Mountains northeast of Silverthorne. The starting point for the hike is at the east edge of Silverthorne near Interstate 70.

Drive Interstate 70 to exit number 205 at Silverthorne. Proceed north on Colorado 9 to Tanglewood Lane, the first road on the right north of the interstate highway service road. After driving a quarter mile on Tanglewood Lane, turn right on road 2021, which generally parallels the interstate highway toward the east. About a mile and a quarter from Colorado 9, as road 2021 turns left up the hill, pull out on the right to a small parking area.

Walk up a dirt vehicle track to the east about fifty yards, then climb the hill to the north. Stay to the right at the edge of the cliffs, keeping a good distance from any houses in the area. After a quarter mile, you join a vehicle track coming in from the left. Bear right on a trail as the vehicle track crosses the east edge of a knoll. Rejoin the vehicle track, and descend a hundred vertical feet to a junction in a meadow beneath some power lines.

Continue directly north across the meadow, under the power lines, because the main vehicle track soon turns east

47

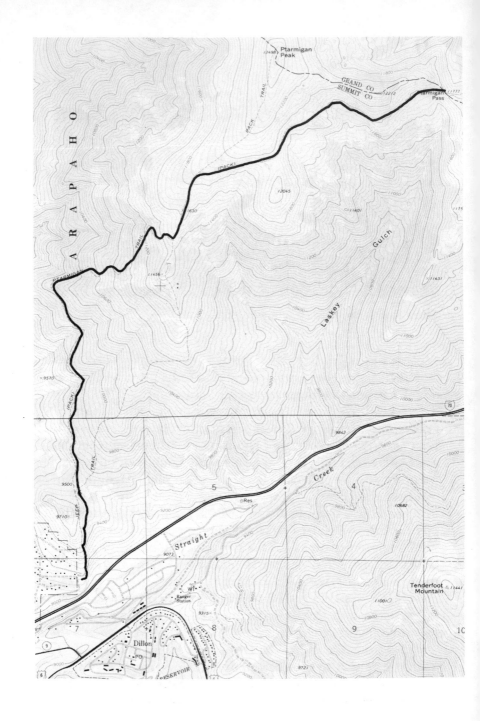

Gore Range from the Ptarmigan Pass trail.

and the route north becomes an excellent trail. The trail continues directly north, climbing gradually. After two creek crossings, there are good views west to the Gore Range.

Two and a half miles to the north, the trail begins an ascent of the ridge to the east. Long switchbacks bring you up twelve hundred feet to a ridge at 11,500 feet. Here you rejoin a vehicle track that takes you northward along the crest of the ridge.

The vehicle track continues north and northeast on the gentle, grassy slopes toward Ptarmigan Peak. The route to Ptarmigan Pass turns to the right about a half mile up the ridge on the vehicle track. Large cairns indicate the way east to a pass between Ptarmigan Peak and a grassy 12,045-foot ridge point. There is little or no trail in this stretch, but none is needed to walk across the grassy area to the unnamed pass.

When you reach the 11,940-foot pass, you can see Ptarmigan Pass to the east, somewhat lower at 11,777 feet. The fascinating view is somewhat disheartening, because Ptarmigan Pass seems so far away. Also discouraging is the fact that almost no trail is in view. However, a trail is there, even though parts of it are narrow and dim.

Look for the start of the trail by climbing to the north. Once you spot it, you can descend to the north side of a knoll and continue along the south side of the ridge toward Ptarmigan Pass. There are some ups and downs, and sometimes the main trail is difficult to distinguish from the many game trails in the area. Persistence will finally bring you to Ptarmigan Pass.

At Ptarmigan Pass you can look southwest down Laskey Gulch to Dillon Reservoir. Northeast is a lovely valley with a stream called North Fork Williams Fork.

The first part of the hike to Ptarmigan Pass crosses private, undeveloped property. The Forest Service has been negotiating for a public-land access. We hope that such an access will be provided before the current private-land access is closed, thus maintaining the right of the people to use the lands they own.

13. Argentine Pass

Elevation: 13,207 feet
Hiking distance: 4 miles
Starting elevation: 11,097 feet
Elevation gain: 2,150 feet
Rating: easy
Estimated time: 3½ hours

Maps:
7.5 minute Grays Peak
7.5 minute Montezuma
Arapaho National Forest

Argentine Pass has been the highest pass in Colorado that could be reached by automobile. The road goes to the pass only from the east side. Four-wheel drive is required for the last two miles. These last two miles have been

Old building at the trailhead. Argentine Pass is just above the chimney of the building.

closed to vehicles from time to time by the Forest Service. So Argentine Pass may be a pass only to be reached by hiking.

Argentine Pass is a Continental Divide crossing between the rounded summits of Mount Edwards and Argentine Peak. Argentine Pass is the highest pass in the state on the Continental Divide, and it is the only Continental Divide pass above thirteen thousand feet.

Even if the two miles of four-wheel-drive road from the east are closed, you can hike up that road to Argentine Pass. However, we suggest another hiking route—an approach from the west. The western approach makes a better hike because it's along a route that hasn't been used by vehicles for many years.

It may be a longer drive to the trailhead for this western approach, and there is slightly more elevation gain than if you walk the four-wheel-drive road from the east. However, for hikers, it is certainly more interesting to walk an old road that is now no more than a trail, seeing

51

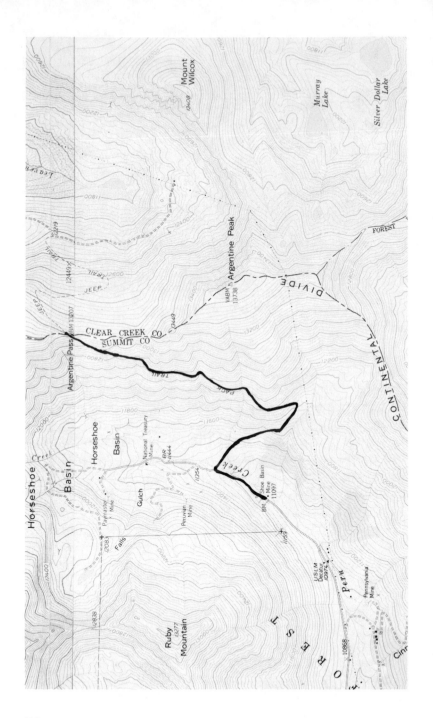

The trail to Argentine Pass. The trailhead is in the lower center and the pass is at the upper left.

where vehicles traveled many years ago, than to walk a recently used road.

Take the Montezuma road, road number 5, south from US 6 about midway between Silverthorne and Loveland Pass. This is eight miles from the Silverthorne exit number 205 on Interstate 70. Follow the Montezuma road east four and a half miles. Just after crossing the Snake River, make a sharp left turn at a "T" junction. Drive north and then east four and a half miles as the road, number 260, stays on the north side of Peru Creek. When the creek and road swing to the north, look for a large, level parking area on the right side of the road, just below Shoe Basin Mine on the left. Park here.

Hike on up the road a quarter mile to another road that turns right and fords Peru Creek. This road goes south a half mile and then turns back north. The route, which soon becomes more of a trail, continues north on the old roadbed and climbs steeply on the west side of the ridge. It reaches Argentine Pass in about two miles. Along the way, many rock slides attest to the fact that this one-time road traversed difficult terrain. Some of these rock slides even make foot traffic difficult.

Two high summits flank Argentine Pass along the Continental Divide. Mount Edwards is north, and Argentine Peak is south of the pass.

For the approach to Argentine Pass from the east, drive south from Georgetown toward Guanella Pass. About three miles from Georgetown, after a sharp switchback to the northwest, take a side road to the right toward Waldorf Mine. Shortly beyond the mine, the road may be closed to vehicles. Walk up the road to a junction about a mile beyond the mine. Keep right at this junction, and continue another mile on long switchbacks to Argentine Pass.

14. French Pass

Elevation: 12,046 feet
Hiking distance: 8 miles
Starting elevation: 10,500 feet
Elevation gain: 1,700 feet
Rating: easy
Estimated time: 4 hours

Maps:
7.5 minute Boreas Pass
Pike National Forest

French Pass once was reached by road, but now it takes a hike to get to the top. This pass is a Continental Divide crossing between Bald Mountain and Mount Guyot. The eastern approach in Pike National Forest is described here.

The route to the trailhead starts from US 285 between Kenosha Pass and Fairplay. If you are approaching from the west, turn left on Park County 35. The turnoff to Park County 35 is about five miles east of an intersection with

The route to French Pass.

French Pass.

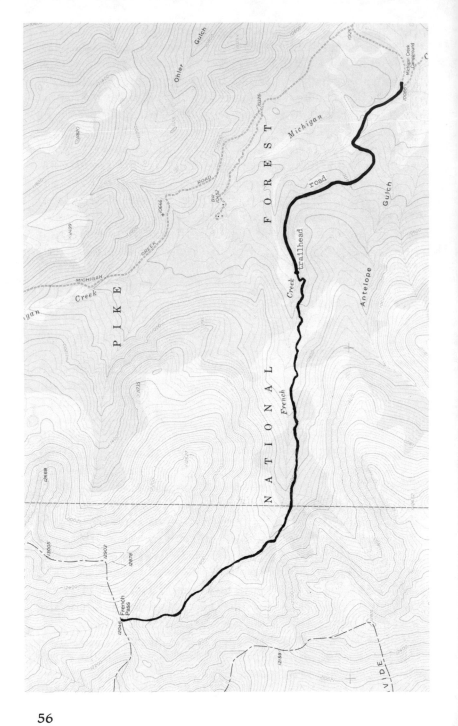

the road to Como. Follow Park County 35 three and a half miles northwest to round the western side of Michigan Hill. At an intersection on the north side of Michigan Hill, make a sharp left turn. If you are coming from the east, this intersection can best be reached by driving three miles on a road that starts out northwesterly from the town of Jefferson.

From the intersection north of Michigan Hill, drive northwest on the winding road, which is Park County 54. This is the route to Georgia Pass, an 11,585-foot pass east of French Pass that has a road to the top. The road has been rerouted in recent years to go west of the route shown on earlier maps. Two and a half miles from the intersection north of Michigan Hill, take the left fork. Pass Michigan Creek Campground in three-fourths of a mile. Drive two and one-fourth miles beyond the campground to the point where the road crosses French Creek. Park in a flat area just before reaching this crossing.

The hiking route starts out on an old road, now closed to vehicles, that leads off to the west on the south side of French Creek. There are more old roads in this area than are needed, evidence of past logging activity. You can see examples of how a pretty meadow can be cut to bits by indiscriminate driving.

Pick out a route on any of several old roads; it doesn't matter which one. Stay left of French Creek, and don't get too high up the hillside to the left. Pass through some open meadows and then enter the thick timber as the route turns north. Cross a tributary to French Creek that flows down from the left. Soon thereafter, look for a crossing to the east side of French Creek, where there is a large gate. Continue north on the single-vehicle track from the gate. You will soon leave the timber.

As you walk up the route to French Pass, after crossing to the east side of French Creek, notice the low point on the ridge to the west. This low point is Black Powder Pass, another pass over 12,000 feet. The approach to Black Powder Pass from French Creek is steeper than the route we describe from Boreas Pass.

The old vehicle track east of French Creek is marked by

View south from French Pass.

large cairns as it makes a gradual climb to French Pass. This track winds through thick willows, then makes a final, steeper approach to French Pass.

From French Pass, you can look north into French Gulch. The ridge west of French Pass leads to a summit just south of Bald Mountain. The ridge east leads over some false summits and then bends north to Mount Guyot. The view back to the south as you return down the trail is across South Park to the Tarryall Mountains.

15. Black Powder Pass

Elevation: 12,159 feet
Hiking distance: 3 miles
Starting elevation: 11,481 feet
Elevation gain: 700 feet
Rating: easy, but no trail
Estimated time: 2 hours

Maps:
7.5 minute Boreas Pass
Arapaho National Forest

Black Powder Pass is the most recently named pass in Colorado that is higher than twelve thousand feet. Its name was officially adopted in 1976. Black Powder Pass lies on the Continental Divide between Bald Mountain and Boreas Mountain and can be reached by a short hike after a scenic drive to Boreas Pass.

Drive to Boreas Pass on the good unpaved road, either from Breckenridge or from US 285 at Como. Boreas Pass, at 11,481 feet, is roughly ten miles from either Breckenridge or Como. The road follows the gradual ascent of an old railroad grade. Park at Boreas Pass near some abandoned buildings.

Black Powder Pass is northeast of Boreas Pass at the obvious low point between Bald Mountain to the north and Boreas Mountain to the ˚south. Walk northeast from Boreas Pass on the east side of a drainage labeled "Boreas Ditch No. 2" on the topographic map. An old vehicle track along the side of this drainage makes walking easier. Pick up this drainage between the Boreas Pass road and the largest building. Follow the ditch northward about a half

Old buildings near Boreas Pass at the start of the hike to Black Powder Pass.

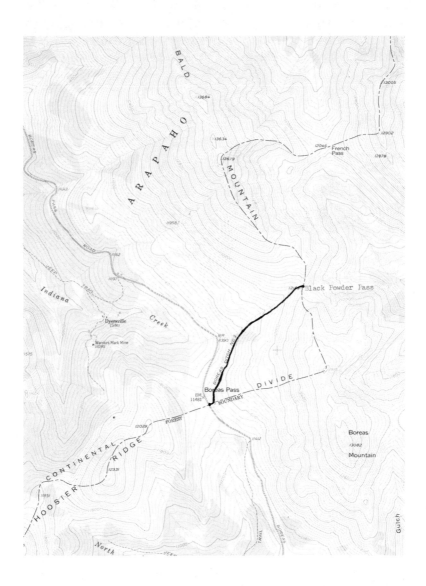

Black Powder Pass.

mile. When you reach a broad valley extending from the northeast, bear right and continue up the tundra slopes. Stay in the broad valley for a mile of gradual climbing to Black Powder Pass, six hundred feet higher.

From Black Powder Pass, you can look east into the French Creek drainage. The route to Black Powder Pass from French Creek is longer than the easy walk from Boreas Pass. The eastern approach to Black Powder Pass could be combined with a hike to French Pass. However, the climb to Black Powder Pass is much steeper from the eastern side.

If the short hike from Boreas Pass to Black Powder Pass is not enough, the mountains either north or south make good extensions. The ascent of Boreas Mountain, south of the pass at 13,082 feet, requires a thousand feet of climbing in a mile and a half. To climb Bald Mountain, a 13,684-foot summit north of Black Powder Pass, follow the ridge north. It is a climb of fifteen hundred feet in two miles with several false summits to go over along the way.

16. Eccles Pass

Elevation: 11,900 feet
Hiking distance: 10 miles
Starting elevation: 9,140 feet
Elevation gain: 2,800 feet
Rating: easy, but moderately long
Estimated time: 7 hours

Maps:
7.5 minute Frisco
7.5 minute Vail Pass
Arapaho National Forest

Rarely do you have a chance to hike to a high pass on good trail in a wilderness area, starting from an interstate highway. We offer two such opportunities with this hike to Eccles Pass and the following one to Uneva Pass. Each of these hikes starts from a trailhead off Interstate 70. Each explores scenic territory in Eagles Nest Wilderness.

Eccles Pass, in the Gore Range, provides a high crossing of a spur ridge running east from the main crest of the range. The route initially follows an old road that has been reduced to foot traffic with the establishment of Eagles Nest Wilderness.

Drive Interstate 70 west from Silverthorne or east from Vail to the exit where Colorado 9 turns south to Frisco. Proceed to the northwest side of the interstate to find a service road leading southwest parallel to the interstate highway. Drive southwest along this road for a half mile to a parking area, where the road ends.

From the parking area, walk north along the trail, which is an old road now closed to vehicles. The trail climbs steeply at first as it winds to the west. Careful attention is required in the first mile to stay on the proper trail. A prominent side trail leads off to the right toward Lily Pad Lake as you near the end of the first mile. A hundred yards beyond the Lily Pad Lake intersection, an equally promi-

Bridge over a swampy area on the trail to Eccles Pass.

The trail as it goes through a long meadow on the way to Eccles Pass.

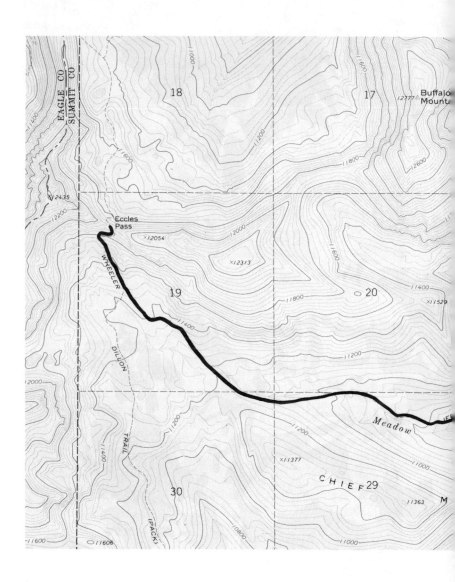

Looking north from Eccles Pass toward Red Mountain.

nent fork goes left toward some old mining operations. The correct route goes right at this junction, winds west, and stays south of Meadow Creek.

Just after taking the right fork at the junction, you come to the wilderness boundary. The trail proceeds west, and in another three-fourths of a mile it crosses to the north side of Meadow Creek. After a mile on the north side of the creek, the trail begins to break out of the timber. There is a mile stretch on the south side of Meadow Creek. From the wilderness boundary to the crossing to the south side of the creek, the route continually becomes less of an old road and more of a trail. If Meadow Creek is running full, you may prefer to stay north of the creek. You can proceed at the edge of the timber, above the willows, to avoid two creek crossings and some boggy areas.

Returning to the north side of the creek, the trail bears to the northwest and soon meets another trail coming in from the left. This side trail is the Wheeler-Dillon trail, which crosses Uneva Pass and approaches Eccles Pass from the south. North from this junction, the trail climbs almost five hundred feet in a half mile to Eccles Pass.

The superb view north from Eccles Pass is into the valley of South Willow Creek. Red Peak and the rugged adjoining ridges may be seen across the valley. Buffalo Mountain is the high point on the ridge to the right of Eccles Pass.

The trail north from Eccles Pass goes down to a junction from which the left fork climbs to Red Buffalo Pass. The right fork descends along South Willow Creek.

The trail that you follow to Eccles Pass in the Eagles Nest Wilderness is a good example of a former road that with disuse gradually reverts to a trail. This seems to disprove a popular misconception that no area with roads can ever become a true wilderness.

The area near Eccles Pass was once considered for an interstate highway route that would have split the Eagles Nest Wilderness. Those who hike in this beautiful area are glad that the highway goes elsewhere.

Eccles Pass, at 11,900 feet, doesn't quite make the group of sixty Colorado passes twelve thousand feet and above. Its southern approach makes the trail open to hiking earlier in the summer than the routes to many high passes.

17. Uneva Pass

Elevation: 11,900 feet
Hiking distance: 10 miles
Starting elevation: 9,700 feet
Elevation gain: 2,500 feet
Rating: easy
Estimated time: 7 hours

Maps:
7.5 minute Vail Pass
Arapaho National Forest

The hike to Uneva Pass provides a different kind of hiking experience. First you have to cross over a busy interstate highway. The first part of the trail overlooks the

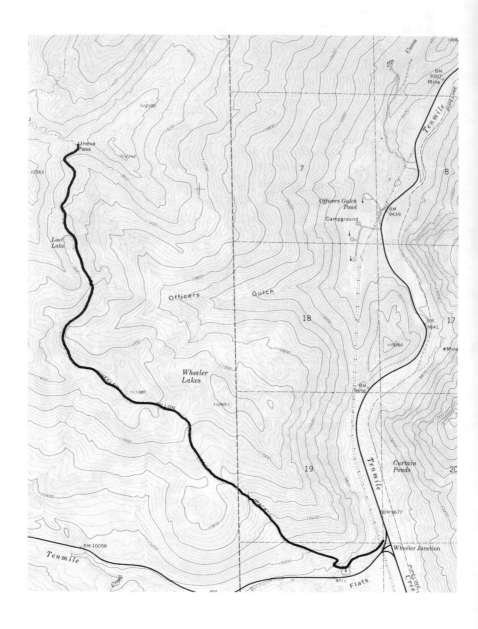

View of the ski area from the trail to Uneva Pass.

highway so that you climb accompanied by the roar of trucks. If you quit after the first mile, you'll wonder why this hike was ever recommended. However, if you persevere, this hike will illustrate how quickly you can leave civilization and get a true wilderness experience.

Uneva Pass is a crossing of a spur ridge extending east from the main spine of the Gore Range. Unlike most passes, Uneva Pass doesn't offer much of a shortcut, since it would be about as easy to walk around the end of the spur ridge as to cross the pass.

One undesirable feature of this hike is the parking situation. Interstate 70 cuts across the southern end of the hiking route, and currently, parking is not permitted along the interstate highway.

From Interstate 70, exit south on Colorado 91 at Copper Mountain. If you are coming from Leadville, turn right off of Colorado 91 just before reaching Interstate 70. Drive north on a service road east of Colorado 91 to a trailhead parking area near a water treatment facility.

Walk west to the north end of the Colorado 91 overpass bridge that serves as an exit from Interstate 70. Just north

One of the Wheeler Lakes.

of the overpass bridge, find a trail starting as a vehicle track, leading west. Turn right uphill within a hundred yards as a trail climbs the hillside. Besides the views of highway traffic, you get good views to the south of the ski area at Copper Mountain.

After crossing a stream to the west and going another mile to get out of sight of the highway, the trail enters a meadow area at 11,060 feet. Look hard to spot a left-forking trail—the one you want to take to Uneva Pass. The more prominent right fork goes to Wheeler Lakes. These pretty lakes set on a high bench make a worthwhile side trip of a quarter mile, particularly if you happen to reach the first lake by mistake. If you do go to Wheeler Lakes, return to the trail junction and turn right to continue toward Uneva Pass.

In the next mile beyond the junction with the trail to Wheeler Lakes, there are some striking views to the west. Mount of the Holy Cross and Holy Cross Ridge extending

Holy Cross Ridge as viewed from the Uneva Pass trail. Mount of the Holy Cross is on the right.

south from it are part of the western panorama.

Another mile as the trail bears north brings you near Lost Lake. This scenic lake may stay lost unless you watch carefully to spot its location above you on the left. A few feet of climbing up the ridge off the trail to the left provides an excellent lake view.

Beyond Lost Lake, the trail has a few ups and downs as it contours along the east side of a ridge. It finally climbs on a long switchback to reach Uneva Pass.

Looking north, you can see the route to Eccles Pass across the valley of North Tenmile Creek. The prominent high mountain directly south of Uneva Pass is Jacque Peak.

18. Searle Pass

Elevation: 12,020 feet
Hiking distance: 4 miles
Starting elevation: 11,100 feet
Elevation gain: 1,000 feet
Rating: easy
Estimated time: 2½ hours

Maps:
7.5 minute Copper Mountain
Arapaho National Forest

Searle Pass is one of the few passes above twelve thousand feet that can be reached on a short half-day hike. It also is one of the few hikes in which the pass is in view during the entire hike. Nevertheless, the approach is varied and the scenery striking.

The trailhead is reached by a public access road through the private property of Climax Molybdenum Company. Drive on Colorado 91 seven and a half miles north of Fremont Pass, or drive south on Colorado 91 four miles from Interstate 70. Here, a paved road, which once was the main highway, angles southwest from Colorado 91. Follow this road almost a mile to a good gravel road that climbs up the hill to the right. After a little more than a mile of climbing, the road levels off as it contours around a ridge and enters Searle Gulch. Just before reaching the head of the gulch, three and a half miles after leaving the pavement, pull into a large parking area on the left.

The trail starts across the road from the southeast end of the parking area. It begins as a vehicle track, somewhat overgrown with grass and brush. The route climbs gradually northwest on the northeast side of Searle Gulch.

The vehicle track becomes more faint within a half mile, and then the route becomes a trail. Soon the trail disappears, and the route is marked by orange flags tied to the willows. While no trail is needed (Searle Pass is evident

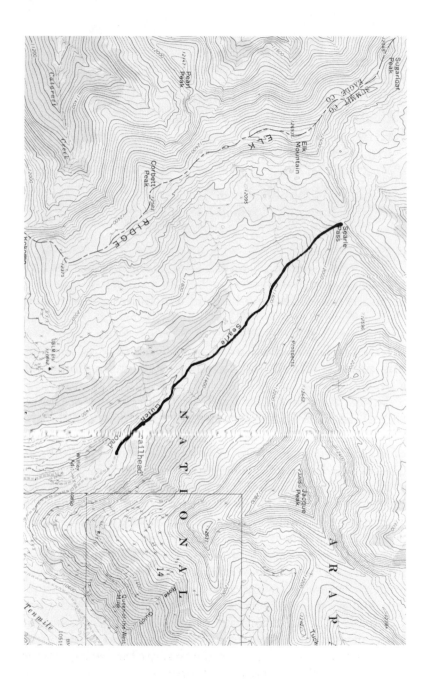

Searle Pass.

at the head of the valley), the marked route helps you bypass the larger concentrations of willows. A mile along this easily followed, marked route brings you to Searle Pass.

The view from Searle Pass to the north is of the main part of the Gore Range. Interstate 70 is hidden in the valley between. To the east, the ridge rises to 13,205-foot Jacque Peak, an isolated high point. The summit of Jacque Peak gives a good view of mountains in all directions.

The ridge to the west of Searle Pass leads to 12,693-foot Elk Mountain. The ridge then turns south and traverses several high points to reach Kokomo Pass.

Searle Pass is best approached in summer after most of the snows are gone from Searle Gulch. The flowers are prolific at this time. Much of the route may be wet underfoot until late summer.

It is a good idea to check in at the Climax Molybdenum Company security office on Fremont Pass before driving to the trailhead. In this way they can offer better security for your vehicle, and you can verify that the trailhead parking area is safe from mining operations.

19. Kokomo Pass

Elevation: 12,022 feet
Hiking distance: 8 miles
Starting elevation: 9,580 feet
Elevation gain: 2,600 feet
Rating: moderate
Estimated time: 6 hours

Maps:
7.5 minute Copper Mountain
7.5 minute Pando
White River National Forest

Kokomo Pass is at the extreme southern end of the Gore Range. The hike to Kokomo Pass from the west takes you into a remote scenic area. The last mile or two require a bit of off-trail route finding.

The trailhead is east of US 24 between Tennessee Pass and Minturn. If you are approaching from the south, drive three miles north of Tennessee Pass to a road angling off to the right. Follow this narrow, once-paved but now rough road, three miles north and east to a "T" junction, where you should turn right

If you are coming from Interstate 70 through Minturn, drive about fifteen miles south on US 24. Just beyond a highway bridge crossing some railroad tracks, turn left almost immediately on an unpaved road. Drive four miles generally south and east. This road takes you along the east side of World War II Camp Hale. You can see the many building foundations and old roads in this area. This brings you to the junction with the approach road from the south.

From the "T" junction, continue east another three-fourths of a mile. The road stays north of East Fork Eagle River. Look for a vehicle track leading off to the left. This old vehicle track heads directly north toward a gorge through which Cataract Creek descends into the valley. Park near the road junction.

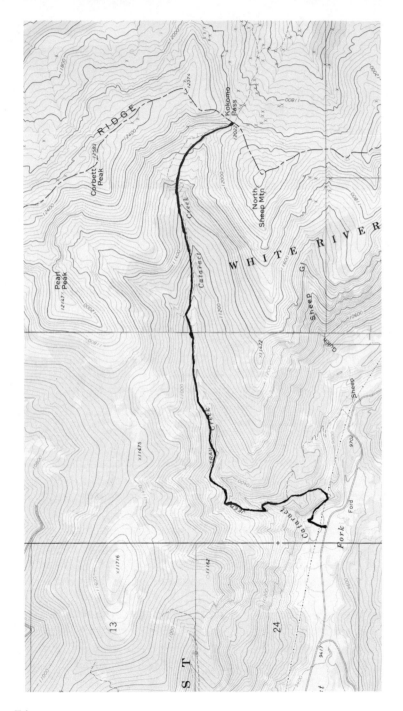

The start of the trail to Kokomo Pass.

Walk north up the old road about a hundred yards. Look for and follow another road that turns off at a right angle to the east and goes through a brushy area. Beyond the brushy area and an aspen grove, the road climbs southeast a quarter of a mile on the side of a ridge. It then turns sharply north.

Continue hiking on this old road. The road meets Cataract Creek, and soon after crossing to the north side of the creek, it becomes a trail. Part of this route is on the Colorado Trail, and distinctive markers may be seen along the way. Another mile brings you to a site that was once the terminus of a road. Foundations and some scattered materials are all that remain.

From this site, proceed eastward, staying on the left side of Cataract Creek. The sketchy trail soon runs out. The route is up through the forest into the basin ahead. Once out of the timber, Kokomo Pass can be seen as the decided low point south on the ridge to the right. The route proceeds up the open basin in that direction. A few game trails are an aid in walking up through the tundra and rocks to reach the pass.

Cliffs near the trailhead for the hike to Kokomo Pass.

Kokomo Pass as viewed from the highway southeast of the pass.

Kokomo Pass is a broad saddle that provides views into the valley north of Fremont Pass. Elk Ridge extends north from Kokomo Pass. North Sheep Mountain is the rounded summit to the southwest.

The approach to Kokomo Pass from the east side is restricted by the private property of a molybdenum mining operation. In any event, the route described here is the most scenic and interesting one to follow.

20. Fall Creek Pass

Elevation: 12,580 feet
Hiking distance: 10 miles
Starting elevation: 10,280 feet
Elevation gain: 2,500 feet
Rating: easy
Estimated time: 7 hours

Maps:
7.5 minute Mount of the Holy Cross
White River National Forest

Fall Creek Pass lies in the Holy Cross Wilderness east of Holy Cross Ridge. The pass is the crossing of a ridge that extends eastward from the central part of Holy Cross Ridge to Whitney Peak. Fall Creek Pass can be approached on trail either from the north or south. The route described here is the scenic southern approach.

Drive ten miles south of Minturn on US 24, or from the south, drive nine and a half miles north of Tennessee Pass. At the lower part of an "S" curve, turn south on a road leading to Homestake Reservoir. Drive roughly eight miles on this solid, unpaved road, one mile beyond a Gold Park Campground. Take a side road uphill two miles to a "T". Turn right and drive north a mile to a junction. Take the right fork, descend slightly, and continue another mile to a

The trailhead for the hike to Fall Creek Pass. The trail leads up the old road straight ahead through the trees.

Holy Cross Ridge frames the left side of the valley on the route to Fall Creek Pass.

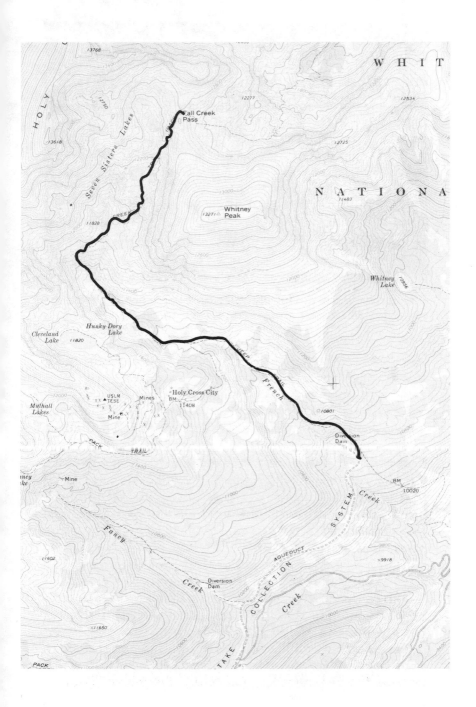

Old mine relics near Holy Cross City, a short side trip from the route to Fall Creek Pass.

level area. Here the road turns left sharply uphill, and a steep, rough road continues ahead. Park here.

Walk up the steep road straight ahead for fifty yards to meet a rough road coming up the hill. This is the four-wheel-drive road to Holy Cross City that starts from the Homestake Reservoir road near the entrance to Gold Park Campground. Turn left and hike along the rough road for about a mile and a half. The road ascends along the north side of French Creek.

When you reach a meadow area at about 11,200 feet, the road forks just after crossing French Creek. The more prominent track goes left up the hill. This is the road to Holy Cross City, about a mile away. For the hike to Fall Creek Pass, take the right fork that circles the left side of the large meadow. A hundred feet of climbing in a half mile brings you to Hunky Dory Lake, set in a cirque to the left. Here you are in Holy Cross Wilderness.

Continue beyond Hunky Dory Lake, now on trail, for a gradual climb up the valley. Within a mile you reach the first of the Seven Sisters Lakes at 11,828 feet. The trail

Holy Cross City.

weaves up the tundra slopes and passes between two more lakes. Through this area there are stunning views of Holy Cross Ridge to the west and its spur ridge to the north. Within another mile, the trail takes you up the slopes to the east and leads out to broad Fall Creek Pass.

At Fall Creek Pass, the ridge to the south leads to a 13,271-foot summit called Whitney Peak. The ridge north of the pass turns west and joins Holy Cross Ridge at a 13,768-foot unnamed summit.

The other hiking approach to Fall Creek Pass is a little longer but has about the same elevation gain. It starts at Half Moon Campground, which is reached by US 24 two miles south of Minturn. Four miles of hiking brings you to Lake Constantine. It's another two miles on trail to Fall Creek Pass.

Fall Creek Pass and Fancy Pass can be combined on an excellent backpacking trip in Holy Cross Wilderness. One good trip over these two passes circles Mount of the Holy Cross.

21. Fancy Pass

Elevation: 12,380 feet
Hiking distance: 6 miles
Starting elevation: 10,100 feet
Elevation gain: 2,400 feet
Rating: easy; short but steep with some route finding
Estimated time: 5 hours

Maps:
7.5 minute Mount of the Holy Cross
7.5 minute Mount Jackson
White River National Forest

Fancy Pass is a crossing of the southern part of Holy Cross Ridge. It is reached by a scenic hike to Fancy Lake and then a short climb to the pass.

Drive on US 24 ten miles south of Minturn or nine and a half miles north of Tennessee Pass. At the base of an "S" curve, find a road leading southwest toward Homestake Reservoir. Follow this unpaved road a total of eight miles to a junction a mile past the entrance to Gold Park Campground. Ascend two miles on a winding road to the right to get to a "T". Turn right at this "T" and drive four tenths of a mile to find a steep road leading up to the left just after crossing Fancy Creek. Park here.

Walk up the steep, rough road a quarter mile to a diversion dam. Just beyond the dam you enter Holy Cross Wilderness. Proceed up the right-hand side of Fancy Creek on an old vehicle track. Then there's another mile on trail. Some route finding may be required, because the trail is dim in a small meadow and in some rocky areas. Cairns mark the way through the meadow. You reach Fancy Lake, set in a rocky cirque, after some steep trail climbing.

Circle Fancy Lake on the right, and climb the steep hillside to the northwest. About a hundred vertical feet above the lake, intersect an old road that once ran between Holy Cross City and Fancy Pass. Turn left on this old road

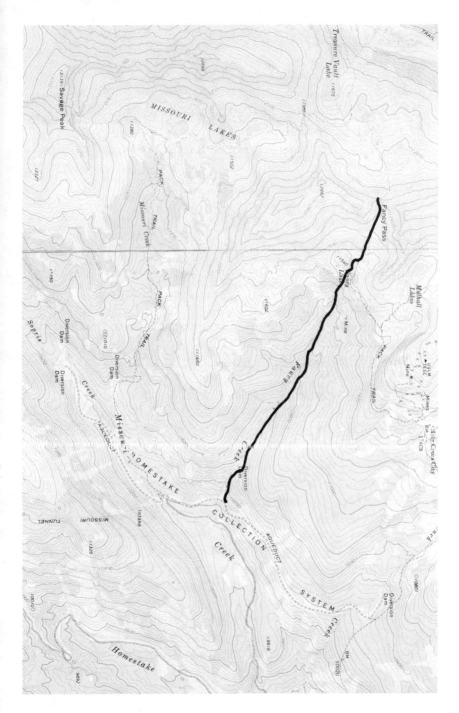

Fancy Lake.

bed and climb toward Fancy Pass about a half mile away.

The basin east of Fancy Pass is likely to be filled with snow, except possibly for a short time in late summer. If the route is obscured by snow, either climb up the snow or pick your way along the rocks on either side.

At Fancy Pass, you can see Treasure Vault Lake below and large Blodgett Lake on a bench across the valley. These lakes are at the head of Cross Creek valley.

A backpacking approach to Fancy Pass from the west can be made on the long trail up Cross Creek. A trail begins at an elevation of 8,500 feet, a mile and a half up the road from US 24 toward Half Moon Campground.

On the return from Fancy Pass, you may want to make a side trip to Holy Cross City. If so, continue on the road past

Climbing to the old road above Fancy Lake.

The final approach to Fancy Pass.

the north side of Fancy Lake. This old road bears north with some ups and downs. Holy Cross City, a ghost town with only a few buildings still standing, is about a mile and a half past Fancy Lake.

22. Lake Pass

Elevation: 12,220 feet
Hiking distance: 12 miles
Starting elevation: 10,260 feet
Elevation gain: 2,500 feet
Rating: easy
Estimated time: 7 hours

Maps:
7.5 minute Pieplant
Gunnison National Forest

Lake Pass was once crossed by a wagon road, but it's hard to find any remains of the road near the pass. Lake Pass is a Continental Divide crossing in the Collegiate Peaks Wilderness. The hiking approach described here is from the western side of the divide, starting in the Taylor River area.

The trailhead is reached from Taylor Park, northeast of Gunnison. Drive to the intersection of road 742 along the east side of Taylor Park Reservoir with road 209 down from the west side of Cottonwood Pass. Drive north from this intersection on road 742 for four and one-fourth miles to a road bearing off to the right. Follow this dirt road north for almost four miles to an open area of abandoned buildings and other relics near Pieplant Mill.

Park near the first buildings on the left, just as the road turns from the north toward the east. From this starting

The trail to Lake Pass.

A lake on Lake Pass. The view is north toward Middle Mountain.

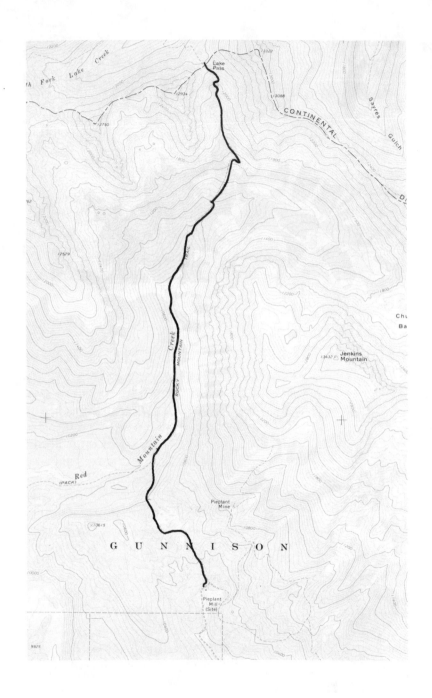

A view south from Lake Pass.

point, hikers can join the Timberline Trail, which passes by some fifty yards north.

Walk north to the right of the buildings to meet Timberline Trail. The well-traveled trail is marked by numerous blazes on the trees. Bear left to climb two hundred feet to the crest of a broad ridge. On top of the ridge, you pass a dry lake and cross a meadow on trail marked by frequent posts. Then the trail descends about two hundred feet to Red Mountain Creek, about a mile and a half from the trailhead.

At Red Mountain Creek, you come to the one trail intersection on this route. Bear right at this intersection to join the trail coming up along the creek from the left.

The trail, still overly blazed and also marked by frequent cairns, climbs gradually along the east side of Red Mountain Creek. After crossing one branch of Red Mountain Creek at 10,540 feet, the trail climbs more steeply through the forest.

Breaking out of the timber at about 11,700 feet, the well-marked trail bears to the left of the drainage as it climbs toward Lake Pass. A final climb up to a bench leads to an almost level walk to the pass.

Yes, there really are lakes on Lake Pass. A small lake sits just south of the pass and another is to the north, barely down from the high point of the pass.

Although you've approached Lake Pass from the western side of the Continental Divide, you have really come up from the southeast on the final ascent. The view back to the western side of the Continental Divide is southeast, into Church Basin. To the right of Church Basin, 13,432-foot Jenkins Mountain dominates the scene. The reason why you look southeast from Lake Pass to see the western side of the Continental Divide is because the divide, as it comes from the north, runs west to east and then swings northeast just before it reaches Lake Pass.

The view northwest from Lake Pass is into the valley of South Fork Lake Creek. Middle Mountain is the high point across the valley.

23. Elkhead Pass

Elevation: 13,220 feet
Hiking distance: 11 miles
Starting elevation: 9,660 feet
Elevation gain: 3,700 feet
Rating: moderate; long, but on trail
Estimated time: 8 hours

Maps:
7.5 minute Mount Harvard
7.5 minute Winfield (part of trail on edge)
San Isabel National Forest

Elkhead Pass, in the Collegiate Peaks Wilderness, is the second highest pass in Colorado. A fine hiking trail crosses the pass. Elkhead Pass is on the ridge separating two Fourteeners—Missouri Mountain and Mount Belford. The pass can be approached either from the east and south, or

The ridge to Missouri
Mountain. Elkhead
Pass is the low point
in the foreground.
Photo by Art Tauchen.

from the north. A traverse of Elkhead Pass makes an
excellent backpacking trip. For a day hike, the approach
from the north is shorter.

Drive fifteen miles north of Buena Vista or nineteen
miles south of Leadville on US 24 to the Clear Creek road,
Chaffee County 390. Turn west, and drive eight miles on
good gravel road to Vicksburg. There's a fenced parking
area on the south side of the road at the trailhead. The
partially restored, one-time ghost town of Vicksburg is
north of the trailhead parking area.

The trail leads south up Missouri Gulch. First, there is a
good bridge crossing of Clear Creek, followed by a stiff
climb on many switchbacks up the hillside through the
forest. The gradient becomes less steep as the trail winds
its way up Missouri Gulch. There are stretches where
willows may be overgrown and may encroach upon the

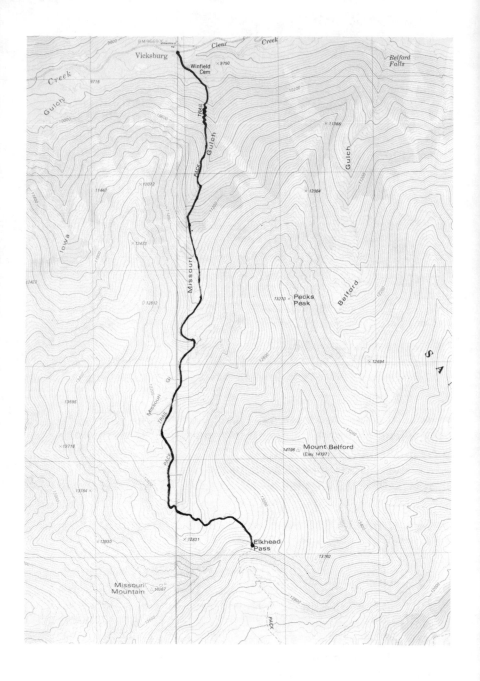

trail. To your left, you pass a northern ridge point off Mount Belford named Pecks Peak.

Continue south toward the pass, as the trail generally follows the drainage up Missouri Gulch. Although the trail may be dimmer and harder to follow higher up in the basin, you can't get lost as long as you keep Missouri Mountain on your right and Mount Belford on your left. The trail bears left as it rounds the west flank of Mount Belford and climbs steadily to Elkhead Pass.

At broad Elkhead Pass, there's a magnificent view of another Fourteener—Mount Harvard—southeast across the Pine Creek valley. A ridge runs west from Mount Harvard to an unnamed 13,762-foot summit. Silver King Lake is in the basin below that summit.

The trail over Elkhead Pass continues on down to a trail junction near Pine Creek. The right fork goes to Silver King Lake, and the left fork follows Pine Creek eastward. The trail to the east down Pine Creek goes by a cabin once owned by Harry Littlejohn and crosses the Main Range Trail on its way to a trailhead near US 24. The eastern approach to Elkhead Pass up Pine Creek is both longer and gains more elevation than the route from Vicksburg.

24. Browns Pass

Elevation: 12,020 feet
Hiking distance: 8 miles
Starting elevation: 9,900 feet
Elevation gain: 2,100 feet
Rating: easy
Estimated time: 6 hours
Maps:
7.5 minute Mount Yale
San Isabel National Forest

Browns Pass is on the Continental Divide in the Collegiate Peaks Wilderness. The hike is on well-maintained trail and offers fine scenery along the way plus an outstanding view when the pass is reached.

The trailhead is easy to reach, now that much of the Cottonwood Pass road has been improved and paved. From Buena Vista, drive twelve miles west on Chaffee County 306 toward Cottonwood Pass. Almost a mile west of the entrance to Collegiate Peaks Campground, and just beyond a bridge crossing of Denny Creek, you will find a paved trailhead parking area north of the road. If you are approaching from the west, the trailhead at Denny Creek is about eight miles east of Cottonwood Pass.

The trail begins as an old road, now closed to vehicles, that leads to Hartenstein Lake. The route starts uphill, just west of Denny Creek, and goes north and northwest on the old road. After two miles, there's a road junction in a level area on the northeast side of North Fork Denny Creek. Here, the old road crosses the creek to the left and

Denny Creek near the trailhead for the Browns Pass hike.

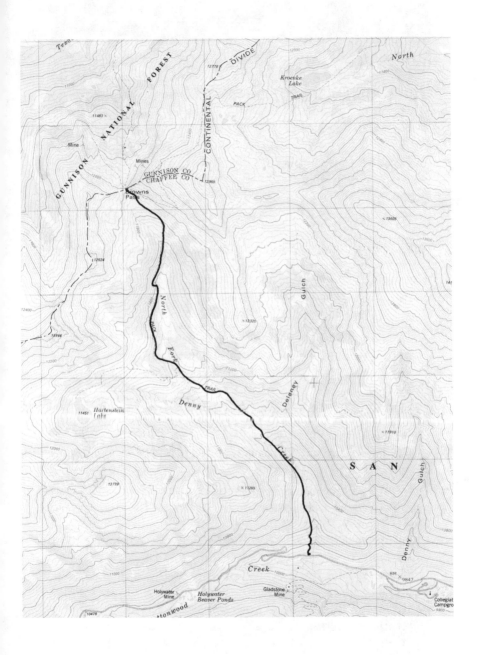

The start of the trail to Browns Pass.

heads west to Hartenstein Lake. The view north from the
road junction is directly up the valley toward Browns Pass.

Take the right fork at the junction. Soon the route to
Browns Pass turns west and crosses North Fork Denny
Creek on a bridge. Now a trail, it ascends the slopes to the
northwest. This excellent trail, constructed in recent
years, tends to become muddy. It climbs the ridge on
several switchbacks to the west and then heads directly to
Browns Pass.

From Browns Pass there is a marvelous view north to the
summits along the Continental Divide, as the divide curls
from Browns Pass eastward around the head of Texas
Creek and then back westward across the valley. The
Three Apostles stand out to the northwest.

There are two other scenic, but longer, approaches to
Browns Pass. One is from the Taylor Reservoir area. From
near Taylor Park, a road goes up Texas Creek, and a trail
continues up along the creek. From the Texas Creek trail,
another trail climbs to Browns Pass from the north. This
trail passes Browns Cabin less than a mile below Browns

Pass. Browns Cabin is a popular overnight stop for backpackers.

Another longer approach to Browns Pass is via Kroenke Lake. From the end of the road up North Cottonwood Creek, a trail passes Kroenke Lake and climbs west to the ridge beyond. The trail follows the ridge southwest and then descends to Browns Pass.

25. Napoleon Pass

Elevation: 12,020 feet
Hiking distance: 5 miles
Starting elevation: 10,695 feet
Elevation gain: 1,400 feet
Rating: easy
Estimated time: 4 hours

Maps:
7.5 minute Cumberland Pass
Gunnison National Forest

Napoleon Pass is on the ridge that runs west from the Continental Divide to the Fossil Ridge area. Napoleon Pass is just west of Fitzpatrick Peak, a mountain on the Continental Divide. There are three possible approaches. The one from the south, which we describe here, is the shortest.

The southern approach to Napoleon Pass begins from the road over Cumberland Pass. From Cumberland Pass, drive south about four miles down two switchbacks to the place where the road turns south after following North Quartz Creek. Find a side road on the left at 10,695 feet that leads to the east and then makes a sharp turn back to the north. If you are coming from the south, this junction is about four miles north of Quartz Campground and about a mile and a half north of the point where the road crosses to

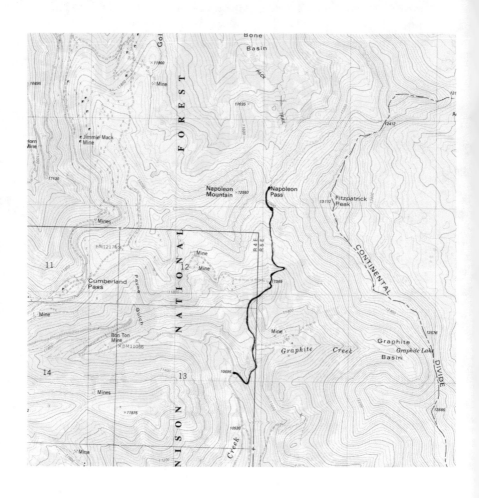

Napoleon Pass.

the east side of North Quartz Creek. Park passenger cars near this intersection. Some vehicles may be able to drive a mile and a half farther.

Drive or walk up the rough road a mile and a half to the north until the road makes a big swing to the west. Just beyond the turn to the west, the route is to the right. Try to find a trail that climbs the slopes to the north. This old trail is not easy to find from the road, so if you don't spot it, head north up the gentle slopes, and you'll likely come upon the trail higher up. The sketchy trail continues north and reaches Napoleon Pass in about a mile.

Fitzpatrick Peak is east of Napoleon Pass, and to the west, a somewhat rugged ridge separates Napoleon Pass from Cumberland Pass. Straight north you look into Bone Basin and the valley of Middle Willow Creek.

The trail from the north to Napoleon Pass comes up the Middle Willow Creek valley. It begins just south of Tincup. It is somewhat more scenic, but is a longer approach to Napoleon Pass.

The third hiking approach to Napoleon Pass begins at Tincup Pass. From Tincup Pass, you must climb over or around a 12,780-foot summit west of the pass and then go southwest to a 12,412-foot unnamed pass. The trail that once joined this pass with Tincup Pass is all but gone. However, from the 12,412-foot pass, there's a good trail marked by cairns leading all the way to Napoleon Pass.

26. Gunsight Pass

Elevation: 12,167 feet
Hiking distance: 7 miles
Starting elevation: 10,030 feet
Elevation gain: 2,200 feet
Rating: easy
Estimated time: 5 hours

Maps:
7.5 minute Fairview Peak
Gunnison National Forest

Of the sixty passes twelve thousand feet and above in Colorado, each has a name all to itself except for three passes named Gunsight. This Gunsight Pass is on Fossil Ridge in a remote area west of the Sawatch Range. It is crossed by a good hiking trail.

The shortest approach to Gunsight Pass is from the south. From Parlin, on US 50 between Monarch Pass and Gunnison, drive north on paved road ten miles to Ohio City. Take the good unpaved forest service road 771 north along Gold Creek for seven miles to Gold Creek Campground. The approach from Ohio City can be reached from the north through Pitkin. Park on the right side of the road near the entrance to Gold Creek Campground.

The trail starts about a hundred yards beyond the entrance to Gold Creek Campground. Walk up the road a hundred yards to the northeast to a point just beyond where the road crosses Lamphier Creek on a bridge. Turn left and follow an old road leading north on the east side of Lamphier Creek. Somewhat rerouted since the latest 7.5 minute Fairview Peak topographic map was printed, the new route now stays east and northeast of Lamphier Creek. This route now has restrictions on vehicle travel. An outlet from Lower Lamphier Lake is crossed after about two miles. A mile thereafter you will reach Lamphier Lake.

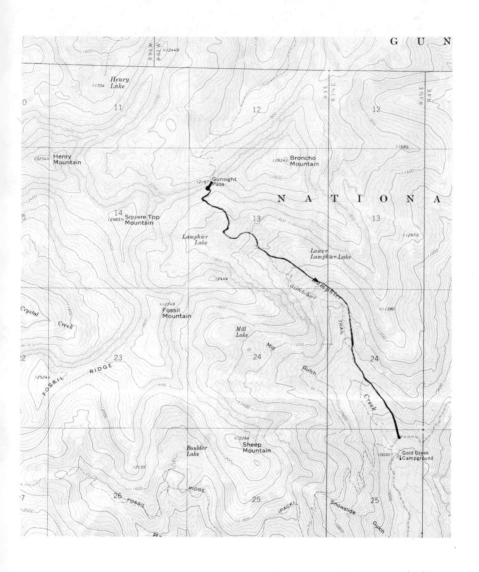

Gunsight Pass may be seen from near the lake. It is the low point on the ridge to the north. There is a very ragged ridge running left from Gunsight Pass. The trail beyond the lake may be indistinct in spots, but with Gunsight Pass in view, the general route is obvious. In the meadows north of Lamphier Lake, some large posts help mark the way.

As you climb into Gunsight Pass and then stand in the narrow pass opening, it becomes apparent that its name is quite appropriate. The cliffs on each side frame a very narrow pass opening.

The trail continues on down the steep north slopes from the pass. It is narrow in spots and often snow-covered until late in the summer. The trail finally emerges at Lottis Creek Campground on the road between Gunnison and Taylor Park. A hike to Gunsight Pass from the north, starting at Lottis Creek Campground, is more than twice as long as the one described here.

27. Chalk Creek Pass

Elevation: 12,140 feet
Hiking distance: 7 miles
Starting elevation: 11,040 feet
Elevation gain: 1,100 feet
Rating: easy
Estimated time: 5 hours

Maps:
7.5 minute Garfield
7.5 minute St. Elmo
San Isabel National Forest

The hike to Chalk Creek Pass starts at the ghost town of Hancock. While Hancock is a ghost town, it is a hub of activity in the summer. It is a starting point for trips over

Barrier that stops
vehicle traffic below
Hancock Lake.

Hancock Lake from
Chalk Creek Pass.

Hancock Pass, Williams Pass, and to the Old Alpine
Tunnel, as well as to Chalk Creek Pass.

From Nathrop on US 285, drive west on County 162.
Follow this paved road and then good gravel road about
fifteen and a half miles to a junction just before reaching St.
Elmo. Turn left on Chaffee County 295. Passenger cars
usually can drive the five and a half miles to Hancock.
There's a parking area at a road junction in a flat area as the
road curves to the right of some abandoned buildings.

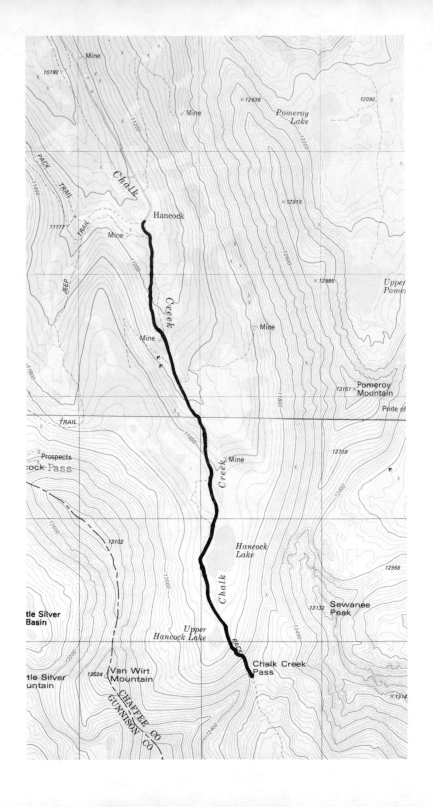

Middle Fork South
Arkansas River
valley from Chalk
Creek Pass.

From the parking area, roads lead both south and west. The route west goes to Williams Pass and the Old Alpine Tunnel. The route south is for those going to Hancock Pass, Hancock Lake, and Chalk Creek Pass.

From the parking area at Hancock, walk directly south along the road. In about a hundred yards, you reach a junction at which the road to the right goes west up the hill toward Hancock Pass. Follow the left fork south, skirting some mine buildings within the first mile. Continue south along the road, avoiding numerous bogs if you are there when it's wet underfoot. After a mile and a half, when you come to a barrier stopping vehicles, you have almost reached Hancock Lake. Continue on trail to the lake, which is at an elevation of 11,660 feet. At the lake, there is often a gathering of fishermen. The impressive broad saddle south of the lake is Chalk Creek Pass.

Walk right around the west side of Hancock Lake, and continue toward Upper Hancock Lake. The trail passes left of Upper Hancock Lake, which is much smaller than Hancock Lake. The trail then proceeds on switchbacks up the grassy slopes to Chalk Creek Pass.

From Chalk Creek Pass, you have an attractive view into the drainage of Middle Fork South Arkansas River.

Although Chalk Creek Pass is not on the Continental Divide, it is a crossing of a ridge that runs east from the divide. Van Wirt Mountain and a higher unnamed summit are along the divide to the right. Hancock Pass is just north of these two mountains. Monumental Peak is the next high point on the Continental Divide south of Van Wirt Mountain.

A hike to Chalk Creek Pass from the South Arkansas River valley would be longer than the one from Hancock. You would start at the west edge of Garfield on US 50. The route up Middle Fork South Arkansas River often is quite wet in early summer.

28. Venable Pass

Elevation: 12,780 feet
Hiking distance: 13 miles
Starting elevation: 8,800 feet
Elevation gain: 4,500 feet
Rating: moderate; long, but all on trail
Estimated time: 10 hours

Maps:
7.5 minute Rito Alto Peak
7.5 minute Horn Peak (for loop trip only)
Rio Grande National Forest

The trip to Venable Pass makes a fine hike, either when the pass is approached from the west side or the east side. The strenuous hike from either side can be made into a scenic loop trip that is not much longer than returning the way you came. Each hike starts from a campground.

The western route starts at North Crestone Creek Campground, which is two and a half miles northeast of the town of Crestone on Saguache County road 71.

Distant view of the Sangre de Cristo Range from Moffat.

Trail to Venable Pass.

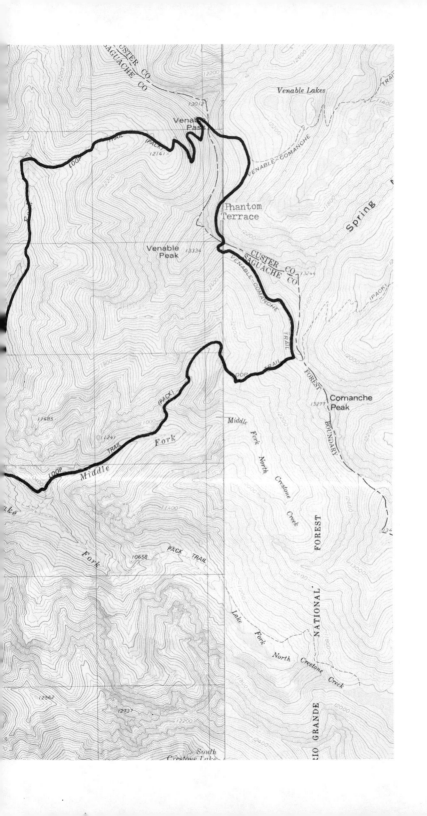

Crestone is reached from Colorado 17 at Moffat by driving east twelve miles on paved Saguache County road T.

From the end of the road, just east of North Crestone Creek Campground, follow a trail that heads northeast on the northwest side of North Crestone Creek. Stay with this trail for three miles. It first stays near the creek, then climbs higher above it.

After crossing a creek and reaching a trail junction, turn left and follow the trail along North Fork North Crestone Creek. Near the junction, you pass two other trails that turn right and go southeast up the valley of Lake Fork North Crestone Creek.

The trail up North Fork North Crestone Creek continues north two more miles before turning east into a large meadow. The trail crosses the meadow and climbs eastward a quarter mile before it reaches a junction. The trail that switches sharply back to the left would take you to Rito Alto Lake or Hermit Pass. The route to Venable Pass continues east up the valley. After reaching a basin at 12,100 feet, it climbs the steep ridge on switchbacks to Venable Pass.

From Venable Pass, the marvelous view eastward is down to Venable Lakes and the valley of Venable Creek. Eureka Mountain is along the ridge to the northwest, while Venable Peak is directly south of the pass.

While the shortest hike would be to return the way you came, a loop trip affords so much more interesting scenery with so little added effort that it is recommended. The loop trip adds about a mile of distance with about five hundred feet of elevation gain, making the total of thirteen miles and 4,500 feet of elevation gain for the hike as shown in the heading.

For the loop trip, continue down the east side of the ridge from Venable Pass. Within a half mile, and after a descent to about 12,400 feet, another trail junction is reached. The left fork descends to Venable Lakes and on down Venable Creek. This is the approach to Venable Pass from the east.

Our route stays to the right at the junction and begins climbing across a very scenic area known as Phantom Terrace. The trail proceeds along the rocky shelves and in a little less than a mile reaches an unnamed pass on the range crest at 12,800 feet and east of Venable Peak.

From this unnamed pass, descend on the trail a hundred yards on the western side of the range crest. Continue on the trail as it traverses the southwestern side of Spring Mountain. South of Spring Mountain, you reach a trail junction just west and a little below the low point between Spring Mountain and Comanche Peak. This low point is known unofficially as Comanche Pass. At the trail fork, Comanche Pass is only about a hundred yards ahead and up to the left.

From the junction, follow the trail down the hill to the west. The trail enters the timber along a drainage that leads to Middle Fork North Crestone Creek. As the trail continues down, it is sometimes hard to follow. Several possible routes turn northwest on the northeast side of Lake Fork North Crestone Creek. Each route eventually merges with another that leads back to the trail junction at the confluence of North Fork and Lake Fork. Once you rejoin the trail that you originally followed to Venable Pass, turn left along the northwest side of North Crestone Creek. It's three miles on the trail along North Crestone Creek back to the trailhead.

29. Heckert Pass

Elevation: 12,700 feet
Hiking distance: 19 miles
Starting elevation: 8,420 feet
Elevation gain: 4,500 feet
Rating: difficult
Estimated time: two-day or three-day backpack

Maps:
7.5 minute Capitol Peak
7.5 minute Snowmass Mountain
White River National Forest

Distant view of Heckert Pass. The pass is on the ridge in the shadow to the right of Snowmass Mountain and above Snowmass Lake. *Photo by Bill Bueler.*

According to the United States Board on Geographic Names, Heckert Pass was named in early 1959 in honor of John Heckert, who lost his life while mountain climbing in the area. Yet it remains a little-known pass in the Maroon Bells-Snowmass Wilderness, an area well-endowed with scenic high passes. Perhaps one reason is because Heckert Pass isn't on a popular backpacking route. It is a low point on the ridge separating Snowmass Lake from the Pierre Lakes area. Each of these areas can be reached by trail without climbing over Heckert Pass. Furthermore, Heckert Pass is not the easiest ridge crossing between these two areas.

If you want to reach Heckert Pass on a day hike, be prepared for an extremely long day. It's better as a backpacking trip. You start by hiking to Snowmass Lake, a popular camping area in the Maroon Bells-Snowmass Wilderness.

On Colorado 82, drive fourteen miles northwest of Aspen or four miles southeast of Basalt to the village of

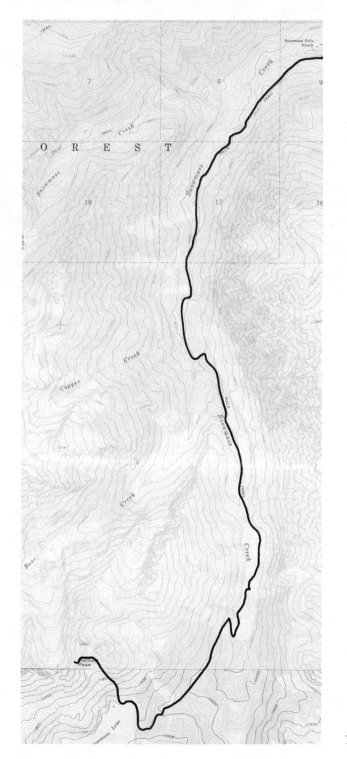

Snowmass. Drive south ten miles to Snowmass Creek Campground, and continue a mile farther to the trailhead parking area at the road end. A shorter but rougher approach from Aspen is via Snowmass Village and then west over a ridge.

Hike up a vehicle track and then on trail on the east side of Snowmass Creek. Soon you enter the Maroon Bells-Snowmass Wilderness. It's about eight miles on good trail with an elevation gain of some 2,800 feet to Snowmass Lake. After five miles, you reach some large beaver ponds. There's a long crossing to the west side of Snowmass Creek that can be made on a large beaver dam.

The last two miles to Snowmass Lake are the steepest. Circle to the right at Snowmass Lake for the approach to Heckert Pass.

Heckert Pass isn't visible from Snowmass Lake. The off-trail route is directly north-northwest from the lake. Round the lake to its north side, and walk west along the shore to a peninsula that juts southwest. Head up the steep slopes to the north.

First climb steeply through and around some brushy timber. Then continue up the steep, rocky slope on the right-hand side of a large gully. Bear west to stay left of a spur ridge that projects to the southeast. Continue up the rocky slope, and head directly north toward a grassy pass at 12,540 feet. This grassy pass is between a 12,902-foot summit and a ridge extending eastward.

Heckert Pass is to the left, south of the 12,902-foot summit. It is the low point on the ragged rocky ridge. About one hundred feet below the 12,540-foot grassy pass, bear left and head directly for Heckert Pass. The final climb requires some clambering over rocky ledges and through minor gullies. As you approach Heckert Pass, and at the pass, be cautious because there are some exposed rocky ledges.

The tremendous view to the west from Heckert Pass is across the basin to Capitol Peak, with Pierre Lakes in the foreground. It would be a very steep descent down the rocky west side of the ridge from Heckert Pass to the Pierre Lakes area.

116

There's no evidence of traffic of any kind over Heckert Pass. If you manage to reach it, you undoubtedly will be one of the few who choose to reach this particular objective out of the many thousands of hikers in the Snowmass Lake area.

30. Willow Pass

Elevation: 12,580 feet
Hiking distance: 9½ miles
Starting elevation: 9,580 feet
Elevation gain: 3,100 feet
Rating: moderate, but all on trail
Estimated time: 7½ hours
Maps:
7.5 minute Maroon Bells
White River National Forest

The route to Willow Pass is all on good hiking trail. The trailhead is at Maroon Lake, which is served by paved road. Few hikes offer as much magnificent scenery as this trip in the Maroon Bells-Snowmass Wilderness.

To reach the trailhead, drive on Colorado 82 a half mile west of the Castle Creek bridge in Aspen. Follow the road south nine and a half miles to the Maroon Lake parking area. This road is closed to private vehicles during popular hours in the summer months. A bus takes tourists to the parking area.

Walk south on a trail that starts from the parking area, and proceed southwest along the west side of Maroon Lake. After one and a half miles, take the right trail fork west, as the left fork goes south to Crater Lake. The left fork past Crater Lake is a route to West Maroon Pass. The trail to Willow Pass climbs more steeply through the thick

Crater Lake and the West Maroon Creek valley.

North Maroon Peak from Willow Pass.

forest as it turns northwest and ascends Minnehaha Gulch.

After leaving the timber, you come to a trail junction at 11,760 feet. From this trail junction, Buckskin Pass may be seen as the low point on the ridge to the west-northwest. Willow Pass is directly north, but it is around the nose of the ridge coming east from just north of Buckskin Pass. Willow Pass can't be seen from this trail junction.

Take the right fork at the trail junction, and follow the trail east around the nose of the ridge. The trail then crosses a flat area before it climbs steeply on switchbacks to Willow Pass.

From Willow Pass, the trail continues north and east down to Willow Lake, a descent of eight hundred feet. A branch off of that trail leads northwest over an unnamed pass on the ridge north of Willow Pass. There is a trail down Willow Creek to the northeast, but there is no suitable access to provide a good approach to Willow Pass from that direction.

The delightful view north from Willow Pass is dominated by an impressive string of unnamed summits on the ridge that curls northeast from west of the pass. The view back south is even more impressive. You look across Minnehaha Gulch to North Maroon Peak. To the left of North Maroon Peak is the valley of West Maroon Creek, and beyond that is a colorful, rugged ridge typical of the Elk Mountains.

The return route from Willow Pass is back the way you came.

The basin north of Willow Pass.

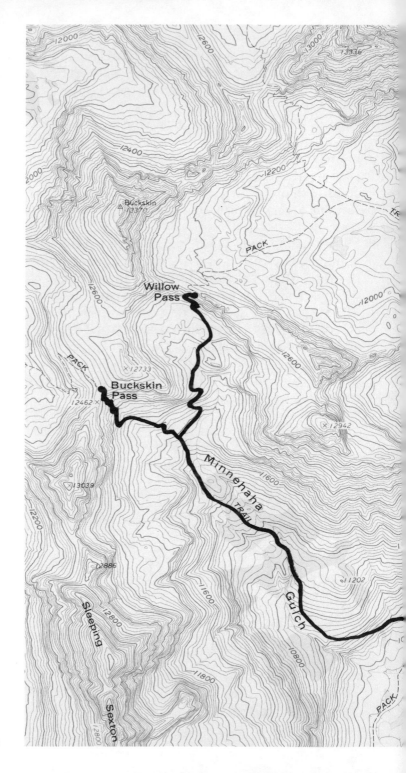

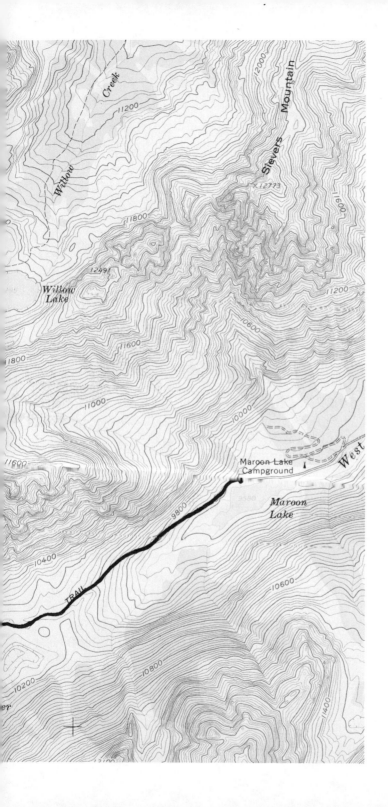

31. Buckskin Pass

Elevation: 12,462 feet
Hiking distance: 9 miles
Starting elevation: 9,580 feet
Elevation gain: 3,000 feet
Rating: moderate, but all on trail
Estimated time: 7 hours

Maps:
7.5 minute Maroon Bells
White River National Forest

Buckskin Pass in the Maroon Bells-Snowmass Wilderness is a popular destination for day hikers. It is also a well-used ridge crossing for backpacking trips. Much of the hike to Buckskin Pass is along the trail used for the hike to Willow Pass. Strong hikers may want to visit both passes in one day.

Begin the hike on the route described for the hike to Willow Pass, hike number 30. Follow the route up Minnehaha Gulch beyond the timber to the trail junction at 11,760 feet. At the junction, take the left fork toward the northwest. This left fork is the most heavily traveled one. Follow the trail a mile from this junction to Buckskin Pass. You will go up some steep switchbacks as you approach the pass.

The area east of Buckskin Pass may hold a large snowfield well into the summer season. Therefore, you may not be able to hike all the way to Buckskin Pass on the fine trail until late in the summer. In fact, trying to climb up the steep snowfield to Buckskin Pass in the early season definitely is not recommended.

The view west from Buckskin Pass toward Snowmass Mountain is one of the most dramatic in the Colorado mountains. In the foreground, across the valley of Snowmass Creek, you see Snowmass Lake at the base of Snowmass Mountain. The massive snowfield on Snowmass Mountain is impressive in any season. Rugged

Buckskin Pass.

Capitol Peak is the high point to the right of Snowmass Mountain.

The ridge south of Buckskin Pass runs to North Maroon Peak, with some jagged summits in between. The ridge north is more gradual as it leads to a summit known as Buckskin Benchmark.

A hike to Buckskin Pass from the west requires a long backpack. The trail comes eastward from a junction near Snowmass Lake to climb to Buckskin Pass. This trail junction near Snowmass Lake can be reached from the north by a long hike up Snowmass Creek. From the south, a hike over Trail Rider Pass can bring you to the same junction near Snowmass Lake. The trail over Buckskin Pass to the junction near Snowmass Lake and then over Trail Rider Pass forms part of the route of a popular several-day backpacking trip circling the Maroon Bells. If you haven't planned such a long excursion, return from Buckskin Pass the way you came.

The Maroon Bells-Snowmass Wilderness in the Elk Mountains is one of the most beautiful mountain areas in Colorado. The high passes are among its best scenic attractions. The trails in the wilderness are excellent. The only drawback to hiking in this area may be the crowds of people. The concentration of tourists in the Maroon Lake area and the many hikers on the trails may make you feel that you are not getting a true wilderness experience. However, the farther you get from the trailheads, the fewer people you will find.

32. Trail Rider Pass

Elevation: 12,420 feet
Hiking distance: 15 miles
Starting elevation: 9,000 feet
Elevation gain: 3,600 feet
Rating: moderate; long, but all on trail
Estimated time: 9 hours

Maps:
7.5 minute Snowmass Mountain
White River National Forest

It takes a long trail hike or a backpack to reach Trail Rider Pass. However, the scenery makes it well worth the effort to get to this high pass in the Maroon Bells-Snowmass Wilderness. Trail Rider Pass is on the ridge leading southeast from Snowmass Mountain and Hagerman Peak.

For backpackers, there are several ways to approach Trail Rider Pass. One approach starts up Snowmass Creek to Snowmass Lake. This is the route to Heckert Pass. Snowmass Lake is eight miles by trail from the trailhead west of Aspen. Snowmass Lake also can be approached from the Maroon Lake trailhead by hiking over Buckskin Pass. From Snowmass Lake, Trail Rider Pass can be reached by a two-mile climb south, with an elevation gain of fifteen hundred feet, all on trail. Other backpacking routes to Trail Rider Pass are from Schofield Park or over West Maroon Pass and then over Frigid Air Pass.

124

View of Trail Rider
Pass from the trail.

Snowmass Lake from
Trail Rider Pass.

The best day-hike approach to Trail Rider Pass is from
the south. The starting point is just east of the small town
of Crystal. To get there, drive twenty-two miles south of
Carbondale on Colorado 133 to an intersection just north
of the highway ascent to McClure Pass. Drive east on
paved road six miles to Marble, and continue another five
and a half miles on the sometimes rough, unpaved road to

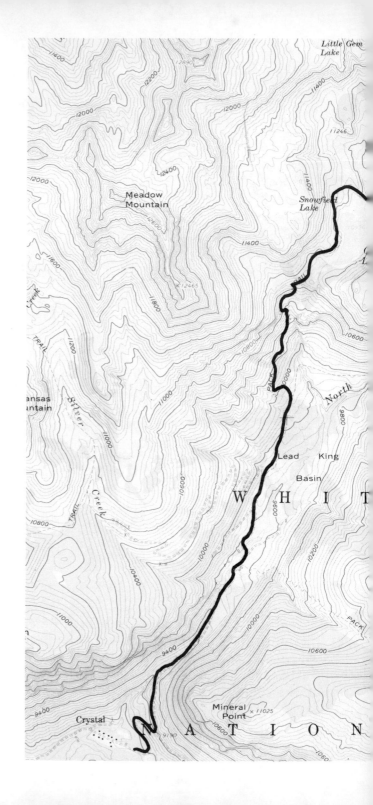

127

Crystal. Take the right fork two miles east of Marble to follow the route east along Crystal River.

Park about a quarter mile east of Crystal at a flat area on the right. Walk up the rough road, making a sharp left turn to the north after a quarter mile. The right fork of the rough road goes to Schofield Pass. A mile farther, make a sharp left turn over a bridge. Another half mile brings you to a parking area at 9,700 feet in Lead King Basin. The route from this parking area to Trail Rider Pass is all on good trail.

Follow trail northward from the north end of the parking area. Within a half mile, you reach a trail junction. Take the left fork at the junction to climb up the hill. The trail climbs the slopes on switchbacks and then proceeds directly north. This is a particularly scenic area when the wildflowers are abundant and waterfalls cascade down the slopes from the north. Some more switchbacks bring you to the west side of sparkling Geneva Lake. There are numerous good campsites along the west side of Geneva Lake for those who prefer to make this trip a backpack.

The trail circles Geneva Lake and crosses the north inlet to the lake. In this area, there are views of the Snowmass Mountain massif to the north. Heading east and then bearing south, the trail enters the forest for some more climbing. It soon breaks out into the open to reach a trail junction at 11,300 feet. Take the left fork, and soon cross to the east of a drainage. Ascend east to a more level area, and pass to the right of a small lake. Leaving the level area, follow the trail as it turns northward to finally climb the steep slopes to Trail Rider Pass.

From Trail Rider Pass, the enchanting view to the northeast is into the upper basin of Snowmass Creek. Snowmass Lake dominates the scene below the pass. The trail can be seen snaking its way down from the pass to the east side of Snowmass Lake.

If this is a day hike for you, return to the trailhead the way you came.

33. Avalanche Pass

Elevation: 12,100 feet
Hiking distance: 9 miles
Starting elevation: 9,060 feet
Elevation gain: 3,400 feet
Rating: moderate
Estimated time: 7 hours

Maps:
7.5 minute Marble
White River National Forest

Avalanche Pass is in the western part of the Maroon Bells-Snowmass Wilderness. This area is much less used than the wilderness near the Maroon Bells and other high peaks. However, it is scenic, and the view from Avalanche Pass is dramatic. The route to Avalanche Pass has been

An unnamed pass at the head of Buckskin Basin on the route to Avalanche Pass.

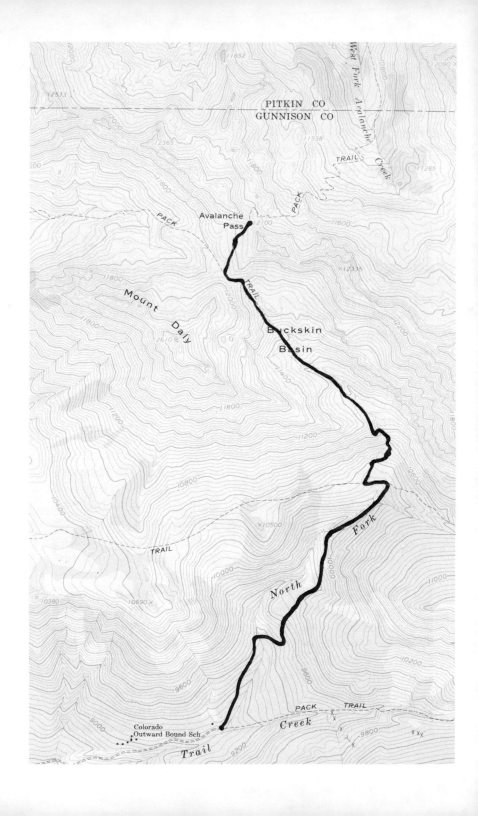

Mount Daly and Capitol Peak from Avalanche Pass.

improved in recent years with new trail construction, providing better access for a fine scenic hike.

Drive on Colorado 133 twenty-two miles south of Carbondale or forty-four miles north of Hotchkiss. Just north of the northern approach to McClure Pass, turn east and drive six miles to Marble. Continue east on unpaved road, passing north of Beaver Lake to an intersection two miles east of Marble. Take the left fork up the hill at this intersection, following the steeper and rougher road along the north side of Lost Trail Creek. The trailhead is three-fourths of a mile beyond this intersection, just before the road fords North Fork Lost Trail Creek. There is adequate parking at some informal camping areas south of the road. If some vehicles can't be driven all the way to the trailhead area, it doesn't add much distance to the hike to park three-fourths of a mile back near the intersection or some place between the intersection and the trailhead.

The excellent trail, not shown on the current topographic map or the national forest map, starts north from the road along the west side of North Fork Lost Trail

A distant view of Snowmass Mountain from Avalanche Pass.

Creek. It climbs briskly for a half mile and then crosses to the east side of the creek. After making a wide loop to the east, it returns to the western side of the creek in about another mile. Here, the trail follows a very scenic route as it ascends a thin ridge between the North Fork and one of its tributaries. Waterfalls can be seen on both sides of the trail at once. A half mile up this ridge brings you to a trail junction.

Hike left at this junction, descending slightly, crossing a creek, then ascending to reach another trail junction a quarter mile west. Here, the trail becomes more obscure, but the route is now clear, since you are beyond the timber. The route follows a drainage north and then northwest into Buckskin Basin. Particularly if you are here early in the season when snowfields are in the basin, it may be better to ascend by the easiest route rather than try to locate the trail. As you get farther up into the basin, the trail is easier to find.

As you climb up the grassy slopes through Buckskin Basin, the route narrows, and the trail takes you to an unnamed pass at 11,900 feet. This pass separates Mount Daly on the southwest from the main ridge to the northeast on which Avalanche Pass is located. Avalanche Pass is in view to the north of the unnamed pass, a half mile away and only two hundred feet higher. The rolling countryside and grassy meadows present a different picture than the one you will see when you reach Avalanche Pass. So continue on trail another half mile to Avalanche Pass.

The terrific view from Avalanche Pass to the northeast shows part of the rugged peaks in the Maroon Bells-Snowmass Wilderness from a direction from which they are less frequently viewed. The panorama includes Capitol Peak on the left and extends through Snowmass Mountain to Hagerman Peak on the right.

34. Electric Pass

Elevation: 13,500 feet
Hiking distance: 11 miles
Starting elevation: 9,880 feet
Elevation gain: 3,700 feet
Rating: moderate
Estimated time: 8 hours
Maps:
7.5 minute Hayden Peak
White River National Forest

Electric Pass is the highest pass in Colorado. It is a crossing of the ridge running northward from Castle Peak, the highest summit in the Elk Mountains. Electric Pass is served by trail that goes from the Castle Creek drainage to the Conundrum Creek valley. The shortest approach is from the east, the Castle Creek side, and that is the side with the best trail.

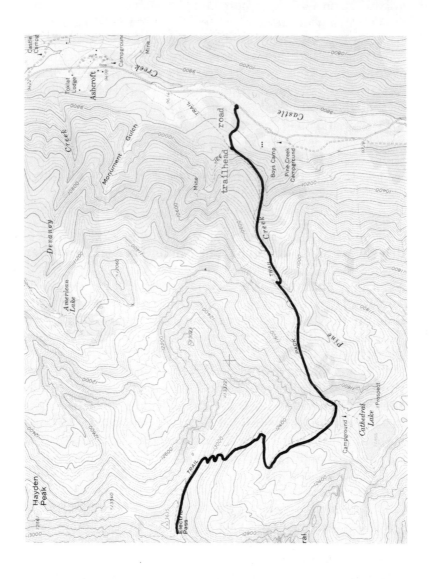

Electric Pass.
The pass is left of the
rounded summit of
Electric Pass Peak.

From the Castle Creek bridge on the west edge of Aspen, drive west on Colorado 82 a half mile. Turn left, and then immediately left again to get on the Castle Creek road. Continue about a mile beyond the restored Ashcroft buildings to a road on the right. Turn right and drive a half mile on this unpaved road. This brings you to a parking area at the trailhead for hikes to Cathedral Lake and Electric Pass.

Hike up the popular trail toward Cathedral Lake. After rounding a ridge through the forest in the first half mile, the trail continues up the right side of Pine Creek, the drainage from Cathedral Lake. After about two miles, bear right at a trail junction to climb above Pine Creek. The trail to the left, which stays in the Pine Creek valley, goes toward Cathedral Lake. As you approach Cathedral Lake in the next mile, with the lake still out of sight, several other trail junctions provide alternate routes toward the lake. If you take the right fork each time you have a choice, you will stay on the route to Electric Pass.

After passing the junctions with trails leading left to Cathedral Lake, the trail to Electric Pass heads up through a broad basin to the northwest. Spectacular Cathedral Peak and its flanking ridges are on the left. Up the basin to the right is a 13,635-foot summit known as Electric Pass Peak.

View west from Electric Pass.

Electric Pass is just to the left of Electric Pass Peak, which, with its rounded ridges, seems out of character with the rest of the rugged mountains. Leahy Peak, a recently named 13,322-foot ridge point, is northeast of the basin on the ridge running southeast from Electric Pass Peak.

The trail turns right out of the basin, climbs on switchbacks to the ridge on the right, then contours left near the crest of the ridge to Electric Pass. The trail to Electric Pass contours high along the south flank of the ridge between Leahy Peak and Electric Pass Peak. It leads to Electric Pass on the ridge between Electric Pass Peak and Cathedral Peak. The pass is at a ridge crossing only 135 feet lower than the summit of Electric Pass Peak.

Electric Pass is one of the best examples of a pass that is located at a significantly higher elevation than the low point along a ridge. The lowest point on the ridge between 13,943-foot Cathedral Peak and 13,635-foot Electric Pass Peak is about 13,300 feet. As you approach Electric Pass, it is easy to see why the trail wasn't built over the ridge at that low point. The rugged cliffs near the lowest part of the ridge made it easier to build the trail over the ridge about 200 feet higher. However, even if the trail had been built over the low point of the ridge, and the elevation of the pass had been recorded accordingly, Electric Pass would still be the highest pass in Colorado.

On the western side of Electric Pass, a rugged, unmaintained trail drops down into the Conundrum Creek valley. It meets the long trail that goes up Conundrum Creek past Conundrum Hot Springs to Triangle Pass. Approaching Electric Pass from the Conundrum Creek side would best be done on a backpacking trip. For this day hike, return past Cathedral Lake back to the trailhead.

35. West Maroon Pass

Elevation: 12,500 feet
Hiking distance: 7½ miles
Starting elevation: 10,400 feet
Elevation gain: 2,150 feet
Rating: easy
Estimated time: 5½ hours

Maps:
7.5 minute Maroon Bells
7.5 minute Snowmass Mountain
White River National Forest

West Maroon Pass is a ridge crossing south of the Maroon Bells at the edge of the Maroon Bells-Snowmass Wilderness. The pass is a crossing from the West Maroon Creek valley on the north into the valley of East Fork Crystal River on the south. For a day hike, West Maroon Pass can be approached either from the north or south. The southern approach is shorter and there will be fewer other hikers, but the trailhead may be harder to reach.

For the southern approach, the starting point for hiking is at Schofield Park. Schofield Park is a mile northwest of Schofield Pass. The trailhead usually can be reached by passenger car through Crested Butte. From Crested Butte, drive north eight miles on road 317 to Gothic, and continue another six miles to Schofield Pass.

From Schofield Pass, it's a mile northwest down into Schofield Park. The road from Schofield Pass to Schofield Park sometimes may be difficult for passenger cars, especially the return uphill from Schofield Park. Just after a creek crossing as the road levels into Schofield Park, the route is to the right, or northeast, on a road leading out of the flat area.

After turning northeast from the road through Schofield Park, you're on the northwest side of East Fork Crystal River. Find a parking place along this road in the first hundred yards.

There's another and more notorious way to get to Schofield Park. This is on the rugged and dangerous four-wheel-drive road from Crystal. The route between Crystal and Schofield Park is not recommended even for those with four-wheel-drive vehicles.

From the trailhead in Schofield Park, hike east on the rough road along the East Fork. Within a half mile, bear right on one of several trails parallel to the road. These trails eventually merge into a single trail. About two miles from the trailhead, you come to a trail junction with the left fork turning uphill. Continue straight ahead on the right fork, which bends right to another trail junction at a "T". This junction is about three-fourths of a mile from the previous one. So far the climbing has been rather gradual to bring you to this "T" junction at 11,650 feet. Turn right at this junction. From here, it's a little over a mile to West Maroon Pass. First there is a level stretch and then some steeper climbing to get to the pass, which is at 12,500 feet.

The ridge north of West Maroon Pass leads to Belleview Mountain, a 13,233-foot summit. From Belleview Mountain, the ridge continues northward to the Maroon Bells. South of West Maroon Pass is another Mount Bellview, this one a 12,519-foot summit with a slightly different spelling.

A longer, perhaps more scenic, approach to West Maroon Pass can be made from Maroon Lake. The starting point may be easier to get to, since it is on paved road out of Aspen. The hike from Maroon Lake to West Maroon Pass and back is thirteen miles, with an elevation gain of about three thousand feet.

With transportation arrangements, a good one-way hike can be made between Maroon Lake and Schofield Park. Without such arrangements, return to Schofield Park the way you came.

36. Frigid Air Pass

Elevation: 12,380 feet
Hiking distance: 7½ miles
Starting elevation: 10,400 feet
Elevation gain: 2,050 feet
Rating: easy
Estimated time: 5½ hours

Maps:
7.5 minute Snowmass Mountain
White River National Forest

Frigid Air Pass, in the area west of the Maroon Bells, is served by a fine trail. The trail over Frigid Air Pass crosses from the Schofield Park area into Fravert Basin to the north. The closest approach to Frigid Air Pass is from Schofield Park. Frigid Air Pass is only two miles northwest of West Maroon Pass, and a trip to both passes can be made on the same day hike.

Follow the same directions for driving to the trailhead in Schofield Park as given for the hike to West Maroon Pass (pass number 35). The trail route to Frigid Air is the same as the one to West Maroon Pass until you reach the "T" junction at 11,650 feet. This junction is about three miles from Schofield Park. Follow the trail to that junction.

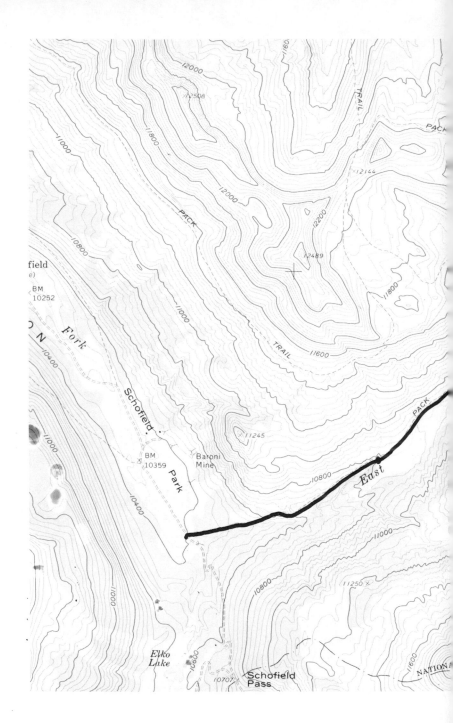

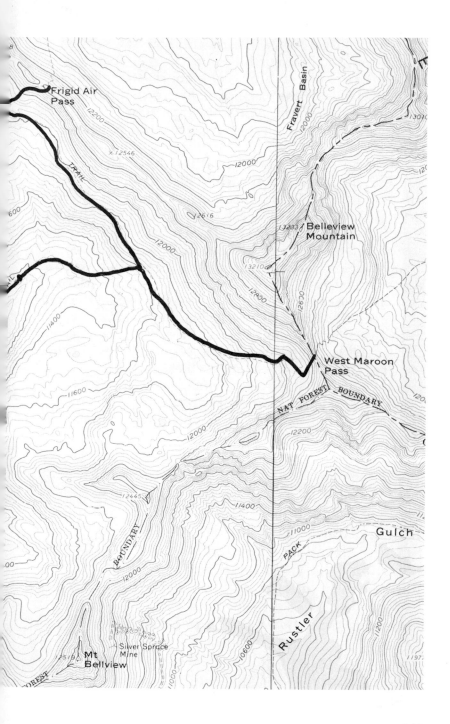

To reach Frigid Air Pass, turn left at the "T" junction at 11,650 feet, and hike northwest on the trail. There will be three-quarters of a mile of very gradual ascent along the southwest side of the ridge until you reach another trail junction at 12,060 feet. At this junction, near a small lake, turn right and climb the steep stretch of trail northeast to Frigid Air Pass.

On the north side of Frigid Air Pass, the trail leads down into Fravert Basin. If you wish to hike to Frigid Air Pass through Fravert Basin, the shortest approach is from Crystal through Lead King Basin and up the trail along North Fork Crystal River. Fravert Basin can also be approached by a long backpack over Trail Rider Pass.

Another long backpacking approach to Frigid Air Pass starts at Maroon Lake. The route crosses West Maroon Pass and descends to the "T" junction reached on the trail out of Schofield Park before climbing to Frigid Air Pass.

If you are lucky enough to reach Frigid Air Pass when no cold wind is blowing, you can take lots of time to enjoy the scenery. The Maroon Bells are northeast of the pass, while directly north is the ridge running west from Maroon Peak. This side of Maroon Peak presents a strikingly different picture than the often-photographed side seen from Maroon Lake.

37. Conundrum Pass

Elevation: 12,780 feet
Hiking distance: 22 miles
Starting elevation: 8,760 feet
Elevation gain: 4,300 feet
Rating: very difficult as a day hike; moderate backpack
Estimated time: two-day or three-day backpack

Maps:
7.5 minute Maroon Bells
7.5 minute Hayden Peak
White River National Forest

Conundrum Pass is not an easy pass to reach, and one difficult part of the venture may be to figure out exactly where the pass is located. That's because "Conundrum Pass" has been used for more than one pass in the same general area, and many maps and reference books aren't too helpful in clearing up the confusion.

At the head of the long valley through which Conundrum Creek flows, there are now three officially named passes. To the west, on the right as you reach the head of the valley, is the pass now officially designated as Conundrum Pass. It provides a ridge-crossing into the valley of East Maroon Creek.

Straight ahead up the Conundrum Creek valley is Coffeepot Pass. It is a crossing into the valley of West Brush Creek, a valley that can be approached from Colorado 135 south of Crested Butte. Between Conundrum Pass and Coffeepot Pass is Triangle Pass, the pass

Conundrum Pass.

View west from Conundrum Pass.

that is crossed by the Conundrum Creek trail. Triangle Pass was once called Conundrum Pass. It permits passage from the Conundrum Creek valley into the Copper Creek drainage.

The fourth pass in the area is Copper Pass, yet another pass that has been referred to as Conundrum Pass. Copper Pass is about a mile northwest of Triangle Pass. It provides a crossing from the Copper Creek valley into the East Maroon Creek drainage.

Conundrum Pass is difficult to reach on a day hike. You can approach it by starting at Gothic and hiking over either Copper Pass or Triangle Pass. More direct approaches require even longer hikes up either the East Maroon Creek or Conundrum Creek valleys. We think that a backpack up Conundrum Creek makes the best approach to Conundrum Pass.

From the Castle Creek bridge in the west part of Aspen, drive a half mile west on Colorado 82. Turn left and then left again to get on the Castle Creek road to Ashcroft. Follow this road for five miles to a spur road, number 15B,

The upper Conundrum Creek valley from Conundrum Pass.

leading off to the right. Follow this road a mile and a quarter to a trailhead parking area.

The Conundrum Hot Springs area makes a reasonable goal for a one-day backpack. You will probably find other backpackers on this route, because the Conundrum Hot Springs area is a popular camping spot. From the trailhead, it's about nine miles, with an elevation gain of about twenty-six hundred feet, to Conundrum Hot Springs. The route in the Maroon Bells-Snowmass Wilderness follows Conundrum Creek closely, so the elevation gain is well distributed along the way. The trail is good, but the last two of the three crossings of Conundrum Creek may be difficult if the creek is running full.

Good, well-marked campsites may be found near Conundrum Hot Springs. The hot springs are along Conundrum Creek and less than a half mile beyond the last trees.

From a campsite near Conundrum Hot Springs, continue up the trail toward Triangle Pass. After about a mile from the hot springs, at an elevation of about twelve

145

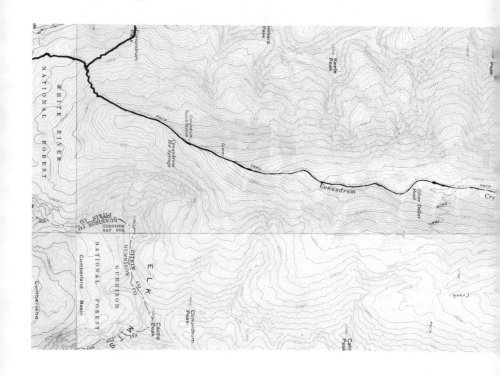

thousand feet, leave the trail on the right. The route to Conundrum Pass is almost directly northwest. There is no trail. Climb over the tundra and rocks northwest to an area just east of the pass. You may be able to pick up an old trail or a game trail for the final climb as you near the pass.

From Conundrum Pass, the awe-inspiring view to the west is into the head of East Maroon Creek valley. Copper Pass can be seen lower down the ridge to the southwest beyond a 13,216-foot summit. The ridge extends westward from Copper Pass to East Maroon Pass, a still lower pass. Look sharply to see a trail from East Maroon Pass that leads down into the valley of East Maroon Creek. A steep descent from Conundrum Pass on the west side would take you to the trail that leads up East Maroon Creek to Copper Pass.

38. Coffeepot Pass

Elevation: 12,740 feet
Hiking distance: 23 miles
Starting elevation: 8,760 feet
Elevation gain: 4,300 feet
Rating: very difficult as a day hike; moderate backpack
Estimated time: two-day or three-day backpack

Maps:
7.5 minute Gothic
7.5 minute Hayden Peak
7.5 minute Maroon Bells
White River National Forest

Like Conundrum Pass, Coffeepot Pass is difficult to reach on a day hike. Each of several possible approaches is a

On the Conundrum Creek trail.

long trek in the Maroon Bells-Snowmass Wilderness. The most enjoyable trip to Coffeepot Pass is by backpack up the Conundrum Creek valley.

Follow the route description to a campsite near Conundrum Hot Springs as described for the trip to Conundrum Pass (pass number 37). From camp, continue beyond Conundrum Hot Springs on the trail toward Triangle Pass. As you approach the head of the valley, Coffeepot Pass is straight ahead to the south, while Triangle Pass is to the right, or southwest. Climb on switchbacks as the trail takes you toward both Coffeepot Pass and Triangle Pass. At about 12,540 feet, where the trail turns from south to west and crosses a level area, leave the trail on the left.

Work directly south toward the broad saddle on the ridge. The climbing is relatively easy over the tundra and rocks. Before late summer, you may need to climb over or around a large snowfield that sits north of Coffeepot Pass.

At broad, flat Coffeepot Pass you can look south into the beautiful valley of West Brush Creek. Teocalli Mountain is the high point two miles down the ridge to the left.

Coffeepot Pass.

An alternate approach might be made to Coffeepot Pass up West Brush Creek. This would be a long and tough climb up a brushy and rocky valley with little or no trail.

From Triangle Pass you could contour directly across the south slopes of Conundrum Creek basin to get to Coffeepot Pass. However, the slopes may hold steep snowfields. A safer route to follow is to go down the trail toward Conundrum Creek and work back up to Coffeepot Pass where the slopes are more gradual.

39. Copper Pass

Elevation: 12,580 feet
Hiking distance: 15 miles
Starting elevation: 9,450 feet
Elevation gain: 3,150 feet
Rating: moderate
Estimated time: 9 hours

Maps:
7.5 minute Gothic
7.5 minute Maroon Bells (portion of trail barely on edge)
Gunnison National Forest

If you want to cross the Elk Mountains north to south, between Aspen and Crested Butte, you will need to go over at least one high pass. One route takes you over Copper Pass in the heart of the Maroon Bells-Snowmass Wilderness.

An approach to Copper Pass from the north is up the long valley of East Maroon Creek. At the head of the valley, the trail splits, with the right fork leading over lower East Maroon Pass and the left fork crossing Copper Pass. The route to Copper Pass described here is from the south—a shorter hike than the northern approach up East Maroon Creek.

Drive to Gothic, a small town eight miles north of Crested Butte on road 317. The best parking place for this hike is in the town parking lot on the east side of the main road through town. Walk a couple of hundred yards north

Copper Pass.

151

Looking down at Copper Pass from the summit northeast of the pass.

on the main road to a road going east along the side of a hill. Usually this road is blocked to vehicles in Gothic by a locked gate. Hike up the road beyond several houses, and continue past a crossing trail to reach the wilderness boundary.

A mining road in the Maroon Bells-Snowmass Wilderness is the route for several miles as the road climbs along the west side of Copper Creek. During high water, some creek crossings may be difficult. After about three miles, there are several junctions with routes leading off to the left. One road goes to a mine, and others head toward Copper Lake. The route to Copper Pass takes the right fork at each junction. At the final junction, you get onto a definite trail to the right as the last old road goes left.

The trail finally emerges from the forest to circle the rocky basin north of White Rock Mountain. A long pull toward the east and southeast on the rocky trail is followed by a gradual turn toward the northeast. After this turn to the northeast, you are very close to Copper Pass, which is up the slope to the left. As the main trail starts around the basin toward Triangle Pass, a spur trail turns sharply back to the left. Using the spur trail, you climb to Copper Pass in less than a hundred yards.

The view from Copper Pass to the northwest is into the appealing valley of East Maroon Creek. The Maroon Bells and Pyramid Peak are high points in the background across the valley. Unless you have arranged for a point-to-point trip, return to Gothic the way you came.

40. Triangle Pass

Elevation: 12,900 feet
Hiking distance: 17 miles
Starting elevation: 9,450 feet
Elevation gain: 3,500 feet
Rating: moderate, but long
Estimated time: 10 hours

Maps:
7.5 minute Gothic
7.5 minute Maroon Bells (portion of trail barely on edge)
Gunnison National Forest

Triangle Pass is a hub for hiking routes in the eastern part of the Elk Mountains. Since Triangle Pass was once called Conundrum Pass, that name is still shown on some maps. The true Conundrum Pass is a neighbor pass along the ridge about a mile north of Triangle Pass. Triangle Pass is the highest of the four passes in this part of the Maroon Bells-Snowmass Wilderness.

Triangle Pass can be crossed in a number of good circle or one-way backpacking trips. The closest day-hike approach to Triangle Pass is from the south.

From Gothic, follow the route toward Copper Pass (pass number 39). If you don't want to include Copper Pass on

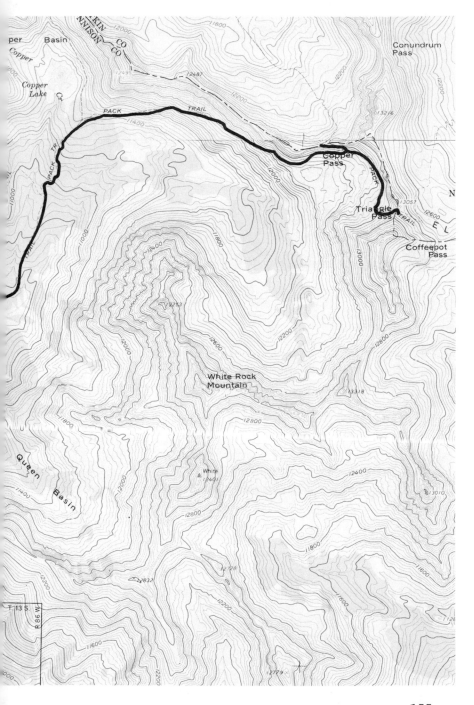

View of Triangle Pass from Conundrum Basin.

this trip, hike on past the spur trail that leads to that pass. Continue on the rocky trail around the head of the basin. Climb along the final long switchback, which brings you to Triangle Pass.

The final approach to Triangle Pass from the Gothic side is through a stark cirque dominated by dark-colored rocks. Just as the trail makes the final, long switchback to the pass, it crosses a small alpine meadow. This is a welcome bit of green, covered with flowers in the spring, after the miles of rocky trail.

From the pass, you see Castle Peak, the highest summit in the Elk Mountains, directly to the east. On the ridge running toward you from Castle Peak is a 13,803-foot unnamed summit. Closer to you and around the ridge to the head of the Conundrum Creek basin is another high pass. Looking to the right from Triangle Pass, to the southeast, you see the broad, tundra slopes of Coffeepot Pass, about a hundred and fifty feet lower.

A good one-way backpack over Triangle Pass can be made by continuing down the north side past Conundrum

Looking down at Triangle Pass from the ridge south of the pass.

Hot Springs to the Ashcroft road. Long backpacking trips over the range crest and back again can be worked out, using Copper Pass or East Maroon Pass along with Triangle Pass.

41. Storm Pass

Elevation: 12,460 feet
Hiking distance: 16 miles
Starting elevation: 9,000 feet
Elevation gain: 4,200 feet
Rating: moderate, but long
Estimated time: 11 hours

Maps:
7.5 minute Squirrel Creek
7.5 minute West Elk Peak
Gunnison National Forest

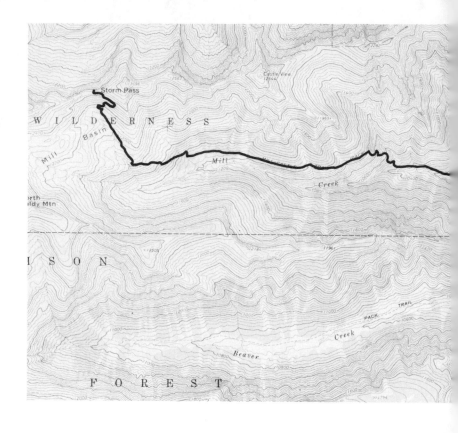

A hike to Storm Pass takes you through spectacular scenic country in the West Elk Wilderness. The trip can be made in a long day, but this is backpacking country, so a leisurely backpacking trip may be more enjoyable.

The trailhead is west of the road along Ohio Creek between Gunnison and Ohio Pass. From Gunnison, drive north on Colorado 135. Take the left fork north after three and a half miles. This is the Ohio Creek road, Gunnison County 730. Follow this road north nine miles until you reach a side road on the left, Gunnison County 727, that goes west up Mill Creek. Coming from the Crested Butte area, the Mill Creek road is about thirteen miles south of Ohio Pass.

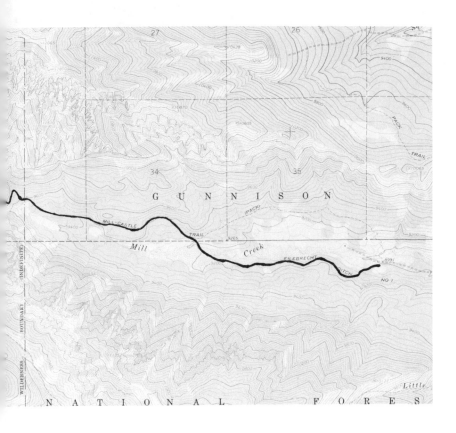

Drive west on the Mill Creek road four and a half miles to the trailhead. The first three miles are on good gravel road, after which the road gets rougher, steeper, and narrower. As the trailhead is reached, take a left fork toward a parking area in front of a gate at the wilderness boundary.

The trailhead and trail have been changed in recent years from the route shown on the topographic map. The new route starts directly west and stays on the south side of Mill Creek for the first mile and a half. It starts along an old road that climbs to Eilebrecht Ditch No. 1 and follows along the south side of the ditch for a little over a mile. A trail then leads north to a crossing of Mill Creek, which may

On the trail to Storm Pass.

Looking into Mill Basin on the trail to Storm Pass.

Storm Pass—with a storm approaching.

present problems in finding a dry crossing if the water is high.

After the creek crossing, the trail bears to the west and joins a trail coming along the hillside from the east. As the trail proceeds west up the valley, there are dramatic views of rocky spires and towers along the ridges on each side of Mill Creek.

The trail stays north of Mill Creek for several miles, crossing numerous side streams and rocky washes created by torrents descending from the cliffs above. A steep section with switchbacks leads to a more level stretch on a high bench just above eleven thousand feet.

Pay close attention to the well-marked trail as you approach some excellent campsites near timberline. If you're backpacking, you may want to follow the predominant trail straight ahead to a good campsite. If not, the large blazes and cairns will lead you sharply right on the trail toward Storm Pass.

Once out of the timber, the trail climbs to and through some large meadows. The route, indicated by large cairns,

The Castles as seen from Storm Pass.

turns north. These cairns lead you through the meadows and scrub timber. The trail then climbs a series of long switchbacks up the steep slopes to Storm Pass.

The final climb to Storm Pass seems rather drab after the spectacular scenery along the way. The pass and the ridges on each side of it are smoothly carved, completely different from the rocky spires on the ridges to the east.

The first view looking north when you reach Storm Pass is a dramatic experience. On the ridge to the north is an area of spires and towers known as The Castles. Beyond to the north is a view of the full extent of the Elk Mountains.

The trail across 12,460-foot Storm Pass takes you over the ridge extending eastward from 13,035-foot West Elk Peak, the highest summit in the West Elk Wilderness. Storm Pass also can be approached from the north by a trail up Castle Creek. Other trails connect with the Castle Creek trail, opening up numerous possibilities for lengthy backpacking trips.

42. Halfmoon Pass

Elevation: 12,520 feet
Hiking distance: 15 miles
Starting elevation: 10,180 feet
Elevation gain: 2,500 feet
Rating: moderate, with some route finding
Estimated time: 9 hours

Maps:
7.5 minute Halfmoon Pass
15 minute Creede
Rio Grande National Forest

There are so many ways to reach Halfmoon Pass that it is hard to pick out the best one. None of the approaches are short. All provide a long hike, mostly on trail. They can be combined in various ways to make good backpacking trips.

A large post marking the trail to Halfmoon Pass.

Halfmoon Pass.

Halfmoon Pass is a crossing of the La Garita Mountains northeast of Creede. There is a convergence of trails at and near Halfmoon Pass. The route that we describe in detail is from the east, through the La Garita Wilderness. This approach takes more backroad driving to reach the trailhead than some other routes, but the drive is through scenic country. The approach roads can be muddy and sometimes impassable in very wet periods.

Drive on Colorado 114 west from Saguache or south from US 50 east of Gunnison. If you are approaching from Saguache, drive on Colorado 114 about five miles west of North Pass to a junction with unpaved Saguache County road 17GG. This junction, on the south side of Colorado 114, is about twenty-eight miles south and east of US 50. From the junction, drive southwest five miles to a "T", where you meet the Cochetopa Pass road, Saguache County road NN-14. Turn left, and go east a mile from this "T". Here, you will find a road on the right, Saguache County 17-FF, leading south toward Stone Cellar Campground.

Looking north from Halfmoon Pass after an early fall snow.

From US 50 east of Gunnison, the most direct approach is to drive south twenty miles on Colorado 114 to a right-forking road toward Cochetopa Pass. Ten miles south and east along the road to Cochetopa Pass brings you to the junction of the road south to Stone Cellar Campground.

Follow the unpaved, winding road south thirteen miles to Stone Cellar Campground. First you climb eight miles to cross the Continental Divide at unofficially named South Pass. Then you descend five miles to Stone Cellar Campground. Drive past the campground for seven more miles to an old road angling to the right. This road leads to the wilderness area. This junction is in a meadow area after you pass through an aspen grove. The junction comes just before the main road makes a sharp left turn and a switchback from southwest to northeast. The junction makes a good starting point for the hike, although the rough road toward the wilderness boundary might be driven all or part of a mile.

From a parking place at the junction, walk along the vehicle track west and southwest. Take the right fork after a steep descent at three-fourths mile. The left fork is the Whale Creek trail. Within one-fourth mile, take the right fork at another junction. The left fork is the trail up South Fork Saguache Creek. The trail for this hike ascends an unnamed drainage to the west, which has been referred to on trail signs as "Unknown Creek." A hundred yards beyond the last road junction, the trail enters the La Garita Wilderness. It climbs steeply about one-fourth mile and then crosses a large meadow. Another steep climb through the tundra and then left of some rock slides brings you to an even larger meadow. A dramatic view of Twin Peaks, a mountain with two distinctive rock formations projecting from a rounded, grassy knoll, looms up ahead.

In the large meadow, the trail becomes indistinct and largely disappears. The route is marked by a series of wooden posts, but some of them are hard to see, since they have fallen to the ground. In any case, head directly toward Twin Peaks across this large meadow. At the west end of the meadow, divert right from the creek to find a trail ascending to a flat area. Here is the junction of the Unknown Creek trail with the Halfmoon Pass trail, which leads in from the right.

Turn left on the Halfmoon Pass trail to cross Unknown Creek, and climb to a minor saddle between Twin Peaks and a 12,086-foot summit to the east. As you descend from this saddle and break out of the timber, you get the first view of Halfmoon Pass.

The route leads down to turn west along the north side of Twin Peaks Creek. It crosses Twin Peaks Creek beyond some old beaver ponds and ascends southwest along the left side of a tributary drainage. Later, there's a junction with the Pinnacles trail, a left-forking trail. The route bears back to the west and climbs sharply. It reaches Halfmoon Pass by climbing up along the northern right-hand edge of the broad pass.

There are many more animals than people in this part of the La Garita Wilderness. Consequently, there are many strong animal trails that may bewilder you, since they are more prominent than the intended hiking trail. It is important to be well oriented and have a good sense of direction for this hike. If you are well oriented toward your goal, the rolling and open country can be traversed readily without following a trail.

Halfmoon Pass can be approached most closely by vehicle by following the four-wheel-drive road to Wheeler Geologic Area. Those who have driven this road say they wish they hadn't, so we don't recommend that route. A better way to get to Halfmoon Pass through the Wheeler Geologic Area is to start hiking near Hanson Mill, at the end of the passenger-car road northeast of Colorado 149 just west of Wagon Wheel Gap.

43. Denver Pass

Elevation: 12,900 feet
Hiking distance: 6 miles
Starting elevation: 11,140 feet
Elevation gain: 1,800 feet
Rating: easy
Estimated time: 4 hours

Maps:
7.5 minute Handies Peak
Gunnison National Forest

Denver Pass is on the ridge between Engineer Pass and Cinnamon Pass, but it is not on a well-traveled route like the latter two passes. In fact, it is scarcely known, even though it is a higher pass than its more famous neighbors. You even have to look hard to find Denver Pass on the topographic map, just south of Seigal Mountain and north of a 13,708-foot ridge point. Of course, one reason why Denver Pass isn't well known is because there isn't a road or trail over it.

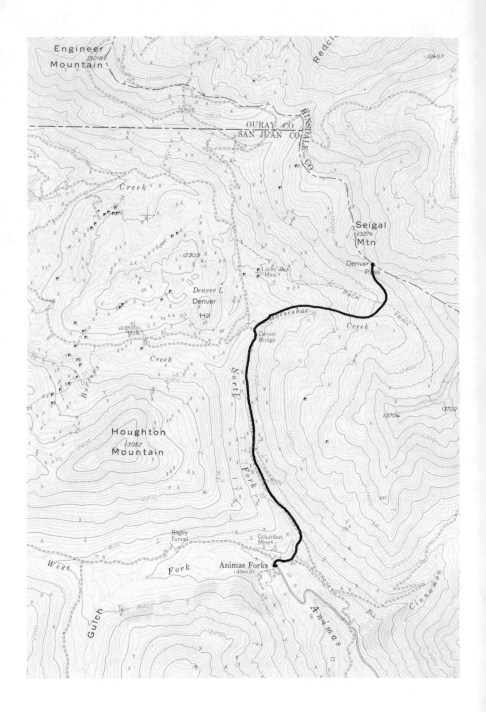

Animas Forks, the trailhead for the hike to Denver Pass.

The closest passenger-car approach to Denver Pass is from Animas Forks. Drive east from Silverton on Colorado 110 through Howardsville. Continue north eight more miles to Animas Forks. Just beyond Eureka, three and a half miles from Howardsville, the solid, rocky road becomes rougher, but passenger cars regularly make it to Animas Forks.

The first two and a half miles from Eureka are along a shelf on the west side of the Animas River. Less than a mile after crossing to the east side, you reach a "Y" intersection where the right fork goes to Engineer and Cinnamon passes and the better-quality left fork crosses to the west side of the Animas River to bring you into Animas Forks. At Animas Forks, numerous old buildings and mining relics make interesting exploring.

From a parking place in Animas Forks, walk on the road to the east. Just beyond a crossing to the east side of the Animas River, you can find a path leading up the hill. Climb along the east side of North Fork Animas River. This route brings you out on the Engineer Pass road near a junction. A

Denver Pass with Seigal Mountain beyond.

road switches back sharply at this junction to go to Cinnamon Pass. The junction is about a half mile north of the Cinnamon Pass intersection as shown on the topographic map.

Do not turn right, but walk north on the Engineer Pass road about a mile to a crossing of Horseshoe Creek, shown on the topographic map as "Denver Bridge." In reality, this bridge is the point where the road crosses North Fork over a culvert. Leave the road to the right, cross a creek coming in from the north, and walk east above the north side of Horseshoe Creek. In about a half mile you come to a multitude of old roads. Continue up on some of these roads to the north side of a sizable lake at 12,536 feet.

From the lake, Denver Pass is the low point directly to the north. Some sketchy trails are an aid in climbing the 350 feet to the pass.

The appealing view northeast from Denver Pass is into Hurricane Basin on the right and into Schafer Gulch below and on the left. Seigal Mountain is north up the ridge.

An eastern approach to Denver Pass would be up the

Engineer Pass road to the junction with a road up Schafer Gulch. Take this road to a point where the road turns east to cross the Schafer Gulch drainage. Leave the road to the right, and walk up the slopes southwest to reach Denver Pass.

Since the hike from Animas Forks to Denver Pass is short, you may want to extend it to visit another high pass. This is a pass without an official name, but one that is known as Yvonne Pass. It is sometimes referred to as South Engineer Pass.

To reach Yvonne Pass from Denver Pass, climb north up the ridge to Seigal Mountain, an ascent of less than four hundred feet. The descent down the ridge to the north is more gradual as you stay left of the cliffs on the east side of the ridge. Yvonne Pass, at 12,740 feet, is the first low point reached.

The return to Animas Forks can be made by following the road down past Denver Bridge to the junction with the Cinnamon Pass road and then descending by trail to the road just east of Animas Forks.

44. Sunnyside Saddle

Elevation: 12,780 feet
Hiking distance: 6 miles
Starting elevation: 10,980 feet
Elevation gain: 1,900 feet
Rating: easy
Estimated time: 4 hours

Maps:
7.5 minute Handies Peak
Uncompahgre National Forest

Sunnyside Saddle is in an area of mining activity north of Silverton. It is a ridge crossing from the Animas River

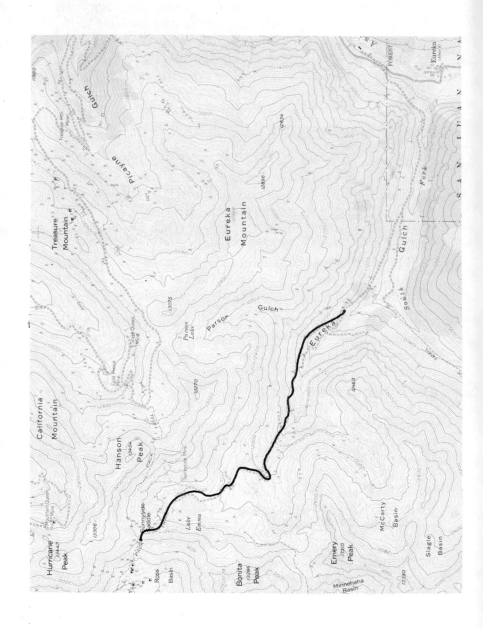

Sunnyside Saddle.

valley to the valley of Cement Creek. This area is not in a national forest, although it is surrounded by the Uncompahgre, San Juan, and Gunnison national forests. Sunnyside Saddle is in an area of beautiful rolling country, with grassy slopes extending high up the mountains.

From Silverton, take Colorado 110 east five miles to Howardsville, and continue another three and a half miles to Eureka. The road crosses to the west side of the Animas River at Eureka. After crossing the river, continue another half mile to a side road that heads back to the southwest up the hill. This is county road 25. Drive up this steep but good road, which leads up the north side of Eureka Gulch. After two miles, you reach a junction. The left fork goes to some mining facilities. The right fork is the one toward Sunnyside Saddle. The road beyond this junction deteriorates somewhat, so we've considered this junction as the trailhead. Some drivers may choose to go farther.

The road beyond this junction may be marked as being on private property. However, the county road extends

View northwest from the ridge south of Sunnyside Saddle.

almost two miles beyond the intersection. Continue along this road for another two miles, with one creek crossing that may be boggy.

At an intersection at about 12,160 feet, with a large, abandoned concrete building on the right, you're a quarter of a mile southeast of what shows on the topographic map as a large "Lake Emma." You're not likely to find any lake there, since it was drained as part of a mining activity. Pick your way generally to the northwest, finding the best route to skirt any active mining operations. Once beyond what was formerly Lake Emma, you also should be beyond any mining activity.

If possible, find a trail that takes you northwest the last few hundred feet to Sunnyside Saddle. Even without a trail, the walk to the saddle through the rolling country is not difficult.

Sunnyside Saddle lies north of the ridge that extends northward from Bonita Peak and south of a ridge point between Hanson Peak to the east and Hurricane Peak to the north. From the saddle, the western view is into Ross Basin. A trail starts down the western side of the saddle. The best return route is the way you came.

45. Blue Lake Pass

Elevation: 12,980 feet
Hiking distance: 7 miles
Starting elevation: 10,780 feet
Elevation gain: 2,300 feet
Rating: easy
Estimated time: 5½ hours

Maps;
7.5 minute Telluride
Uncompahgre National Forest

Blue Lake Pass is one of the highest passes in the state. Most of the route to the pass is along the same path normally followed to climb Mount Sneffels. However, most Mount Sneffels climbers turn off the route to Blue Lake Pass in order to climb the mountain and don't get to this high, scenic pass.

From Ouray, begin the trip to Blue Lake Pass by driving a half mile south on US 550. After the first switchback, turn right on Colorado 361, a road leading southwest toward Camp Bird Mine. Approaching from the south, this junction can be recognized as being on the switchback leading west that overlooks Ouray. Drive past Camp Bird Mine, and continue straight ahead toward Yankee Boy Basin. A mile and a half beyond the mine, pass a side road on your left that leads to Imogene Pass. At an intersection a mile farther, find a place to park passenger cars. The left fork leads to Governor Basin, while the right fork to Yankee Boy Basin is the one you want to take.

Walk up the road to the right. It climbs on the right-hand side of Sneffels Creek and proceeds west into the basin. In a little over a mile, a side road to the left leads to a parking area. Beyond this side road are several choices of road leading short distances west and northwest.

The best hiking route stays left on the north side of Sneffels Creek. It passes some buildings and then climbs up

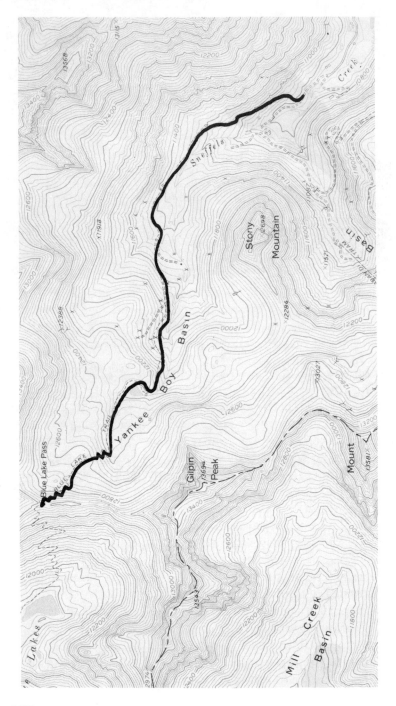

Blue Lake Pass.

to the south end of a small lake at about 12,200 feet.

The route continues around the east and north sides of the lake, which is the source of Sneffels Creek. Beyond the lake, the trail continues west and northwest another mile to Blue Lake Pass. About halfway from the lake to the pass, the route to Mount Sneffels diverges from the trail, and many climbers turn right up the valley to the north. Some opt to head north sooner and don't follow the trail this far.

At Blue Lake Pass, you look west down toward Blue Lakes. The area west of Blue Lake Pass is in the Mount Sneffels Wilderness. The ridge leading north from Blue Lake Pass is sometimes used as a climbing route to Mount Sneffels. The scenic view back to the east is dominated by Teakettle Mountain and Potosi Peak, with the little Coffeepot summit in between. Gilpin Peak is the high point on the ridge south of Blue Lake Pass. The ridge that runs west from Gilpin Peak goes to rugged Dallas Peak.

Despite the large amount of mining activity in the area, Yankee Boy Basin remains a scenic mountain wonderland.

Mount Sneffels. Blue Lake Pass is on the ridge in the left foreground. *Photo by Art Tauchen.*

The basin is a huge flower garden in the late spring and summer. The surrounding mountains and ridges are unusually picturesque with their many varied towers and spires.

46. Richmond Pass

Elevation: 12,657 feet
Hiking distance: 10 miles
Starting elevation: 9,900 feet
Elevation gain: 3,000 feet
Rating: moderate, with some route finding
Estimated time: 7 hours

Maps:
7.5 minute Ironton
Uncompahgre National Forest

A hiking trail once led to Richmond Pass, but in recent years, portions of it have disappeared. The trailhead is near a main highway, but the start of the trail is difficult to find. The trail isn't highly traveled, so you probably will be able to make this hike all by yourself. The view that unfolds when you reach Richmond Pass makes the hike well worthwhile.

The approach to Richmond Pass is from the east, from US 550 between Ouray and Silverton. If you are driving from Ouray, go six miles from the south end of town until you pass to the left of Crystal Lake. A mile and a half farther, the highway turns slightly to the right (southwest) at some tailings ponds on the left. Look for a road leading left alongside the tailings. Go exactly three-quarters of a mile beyond this road junction, and pull off the highway to the right on a gravel road. There is a small parking area at this road junction just south of some mine tailings.

To reach this trailhead on US 550 from the south, cross Red Mountain Pass and descend the switchbacks. Drive

The overgrown trail to Richmond Pass.

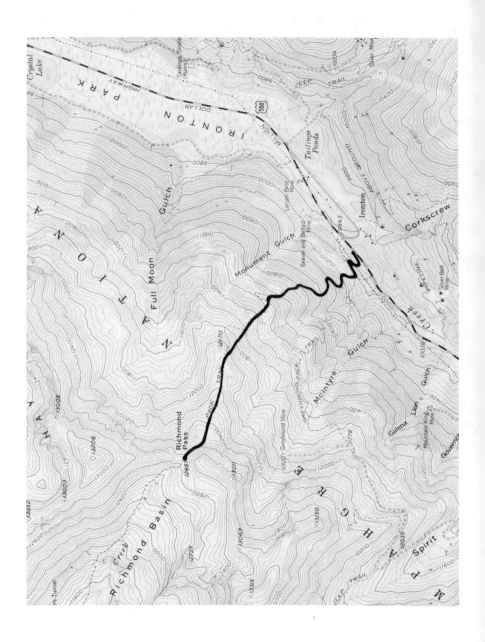

A view of Richmond Pass from the mountain southwest of the pass.

just a shade less than a mile northeast from the south end of the last switchback. The trailhead parking area is left, or west, of the highway. It is important to use care in locating this trailhead, as there are several similar locations nearby. From the parking area west of the highway, walk up the old road to the southwest. After a switchback, the unused road, now overgrown with trees, descends slightly and then steeply to the left. At this point, follow a trail that ascends to the right through the aspen. While this trail is overgrown and shows little evidence of use, it can be followed until it reaches a meadow at about 11,000 feet.

Beyond the meadow, it is hardly worth the effort of searching for the trail. Continue upward along the ridge through the sparse timber until a 12,170-foot rocky summit comes into view. Climb the grassy slopes to the left of this summit to reach a ridge just west of the 12,170-foot summit.

When you reach the ridge, Richmond Pass is in full view. Some stretches of trail leading to the pass become visible. A unique feature is that most of the rest of the approach to

Richmond Pass is along a ridge. There is a final turn to the right for the climb to the pass.

The view to the west from Richmond Pass is spectacular. You can look directly into Yankee Boy Basin, which is circled by imposing summits.

In returning from Richmond Pass, you may not be able to pick up the old trail where you left it. If you descend eastward between the major drainages, you should come across the old trail somewhere above the highway.

47. Hunchback Pass

Elevation: 12,493 feet
Hiking distance: 18 miles
Starting elevation: 10,460 feet
Elevation gain: 5,000 feet
Rating: difficult day hike or moderate backpack
Estimated time: three-day backpack

Maps:
7.5 minute Howardsville
7.5 minute Storm King Peak
Rio Grande National Forest
San Juan National Forest

Hunchback Pass is on the Continental Divide in the Weminuche Wilderness. The pass can be approached from several directions by scenic backpacking trips. In each case, it takes a long hike to reach Hunchback Pass. The route that we suggest enters the Weminuche Wilderness from the north. It follows the Continental Divide south to a good camping location at Eldorado Lake. The starting point is near Silverton.

Drive east on Colorado 110 from Silverton to Howardsville. Turn right at Howardsville, and drive

Climbing up the trail from Cunningham Creek on the way to Hunchback Pass.

southeast and south on the road along Cunningham Creek. Drive four miles to a point where the road makes a sharp turn to the right and crosses the creek. Park here in an area below some old mine buildings.

Begin the hike by crossing Cunningham Creek to the west, either at the ford on the road or higher up near the mine buildings. Walk up the road a quarter of a mile, climbing south on the east side of a ridge. As the road turns west near the creek, look for a creek crossing with a trail starting from the other side. In high water periods, it may be necessary to wade the creek.

The route on trail goes south and then ascends the slopes to the east. Stay left at a trail junction after a mile at about 11,400 feet. The trail climbs up a valley and approaches a 12,302-foot point on the Continental Divide. Bear right and cross a creek to stay to the right of this summit. Gradual climbing will bring you to the Continental Divide. Here, you're about two miles south of Stony Pass.

Head south on the Continental Divide Trail along the broad crest of the divide. After a couple of miles, the trail

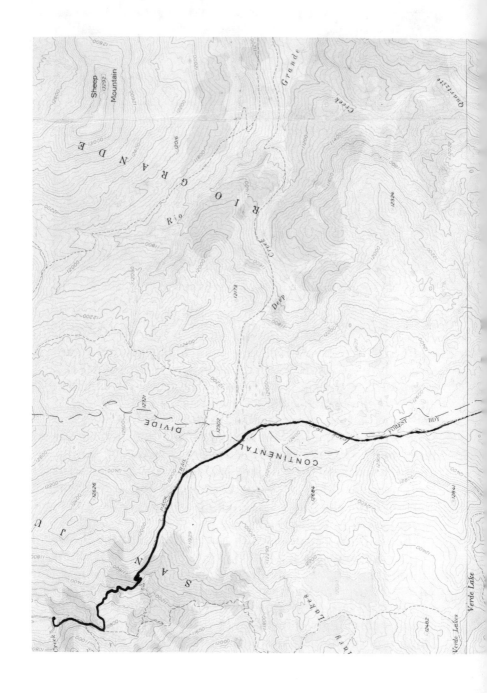

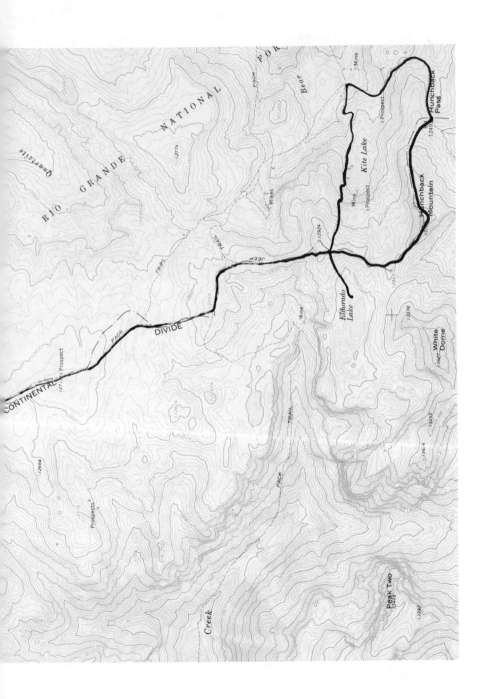

Looking down into the Elk Creek valley on the way to Hunchback Pass.

joins old vehicle tracks. After crossing rounded summits of 12,713 feet and 12,707 feet, one vehicle track bears off to the left. Stay on the crest of the divide. Soon thereafter you meet the trail up Elk Creek which climbs up on switchbacks from the right. The Elk Creek Trail begins at Molas Lake and passes through Elk Park, providing an alternate route to Hunchback Pass. Three-quarters of a mile beyond the Elk Creek Trail junction, just after passing right of a knoll of 12,924 feet, the trail makes a sharp turn to the left and descends east to Kite Lake. To the right, west of the divide, is Eldorado Lake. The area near Eldorado Lake provides the best camping locations.

There are two good routes to Hunchback Pass from the divide between Eldorado Lake and Kite Lake. Each requires some climbing and some descent. One is on good, constructed trail, while the other follows a trail of use over Hunchback Mountain. From a camp at Eldorado Lake or Kite Lake, it makes a varied hike if you go one way and return the other.

Approaching Hunchback Pass.

From Kite Lake, walk a little over a half mile east down the four-wheel-drive road and pick up the trail on the right. Proceed to Hunchback Pass from this junction at about 11,700 feet by climbing on the trail for a little more than a mile.

An alternate route to Hunchback Pass is to continue south on the divide over Hunchback Mountain rather than descend to Kite Lake. Continue down the east side of the mountain to Hunchback Pass. This alternative is attractive if you don't intend to camp near Kite Lake and if you prefer a shorter but steeper off-trail route. The ascent of Hunchback Mountain is by its northwest ridge. The route follows a frequently walked path near the crest of the ridge. The descent to Hunchback Pass is more gradual, without a definite trail.

The route down the west side of Hunchback Pass leads to Vallecito Creek. A long trail down Vallecito Creek descends gradually to a trailhead north of Vallecito Reservoir. The approach to Hunchback Pass up Vallecito

Creek is almost twice as long as the one from Cunningham Creek.

If a hike from Eldorado Lake or Kite Lake to Hunchback Pass is too short for one day, the trip can be extended by hiking south to another pass along the Continental Divide. Follow the trail down the west side of Hunchback Pass. In about a mile and a half, after a descent to about 11,400 feet, take a left-forking trail. This trail climbs up Nebo Creek and then ascends a basin to Nebo Pass, an unofficially named pass on the Continental Divide at 12,460 feet.

From Nebo Pass, you can return to Hunchback Pass either on the trail or by following the rocky Continental Divide. From Hunchback Pass, take one of the two suggested routes back to your camp.

48. Columbine Pass

Elevation: 12,700 feet
Hiking distance: 16 miles
Starting elevation: 8,212 feet
Elevation gain: 4,500 feet
Rating: moderate
Estimated time: three-day backpack

Maps:
7.5 minute Columbine Pass
7.5 minute Mountain View Crest
7.5 minute Snowdon Peak (trailhead area only)
San Juan National Forest

Columbine Pass is in the heart of the Weminuche Wilderness. It is a key crossing of the range crest for long backpacking trips. The shortest backpacking route to Columbine Pass starts with a ride on the narrow-gauge

Columbine Lake from the Columbine Pass trail.

railroad to Needleton from either Durango or Silverton. A longer approach without the train ride can be made if desired. Several excellent one-way trips over Columbine Pass also can be worked out.

For the start by railroad, take the train from either Durango or Silverton, getting off at Needleton. The ride from Durango is longer, but it gets you to the trailhead earlier in the day. With present train schedules, starting from Durango provides more time to backpack to a good camping location before dark.

Cross the Animas River on the Needleton bridge and hike up the trail to Chicago Basin. The trail from Needleton to Chicago Basin is one of the most used trails in the Weminuche Wilderness. Much of the backpacking traffic to Chicago Basin is for the purpose of climbing the three Fourteeners in the area. From east of the Animas River bridge at Needleton, follow the trail about a mile south to a junction. Here, another trail joins on the right, coming in from Purgatory Campground ten miles away. Follow the

191

The trail from Chicago Basin to Columbine Pass.

left fork that climbs up the valley along the left side of Needle Creek.

After about five miles and a climb to eleven thousand feet on the well-used trail, you reach another trail junction in a meadow. The best route to Columbine Pass, as well as to some good camping areas, is to take the right fork at this junction. The trail climbs steeply on the left side of a drainage entering from the right. After hiking a mile up along this drainage, ascending six hundred feet, excellent camping spots can be found in a flat wooded area. If you don't make it this far after arriving at Needleton, suitable camping locations can be found before reaching the junction.

Just beyond the camping area at 11,600 feet, there is another trail junction. The trail to the right goes to Columbine Pass, while the branch to the left descends into upper Chicago Basin. Follow the right fork for a climb on switchbacks to Columbine Pass.

At the pass, you can look down on Columbine Lake, Vallecito Basin, and the valley extending down Johnson Creek. The high summits to the east are Grizzly Peak and McCauley Peak.

Chicago Basin. Columbine Pass is in the upper center of the picture.

For a longer approach to Columbine Pass without the train ride, hike up the trail along Johnson Creek. Start at the trailhead near Vallecito Campground north of Vallecito Reservoir. The first eight and a half miles are north along Vallecito Creek, and then the route turns up Johnson Creek, with the total distance to Columbine Pass about fifteen miles.

49. Trimble Pass

Elevation: 12,860 feet
Hiking distance: 19 miles
Starting elevation: 8,212 feet
Elevation gain: 4,850 feet
Rating: moderate
Estimated time: three-day backpack

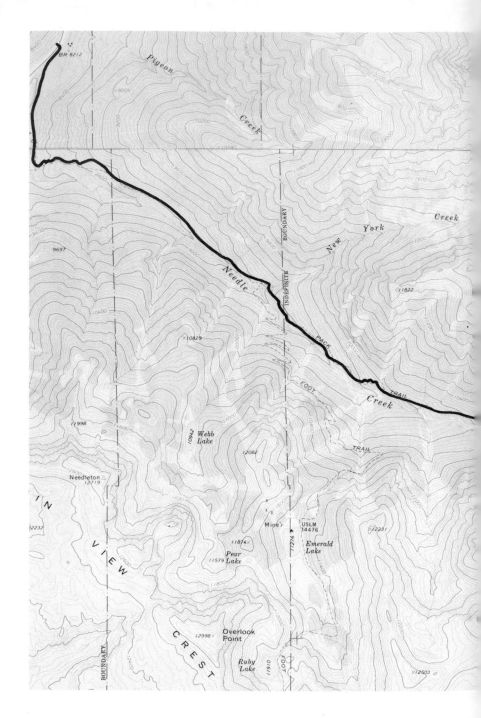

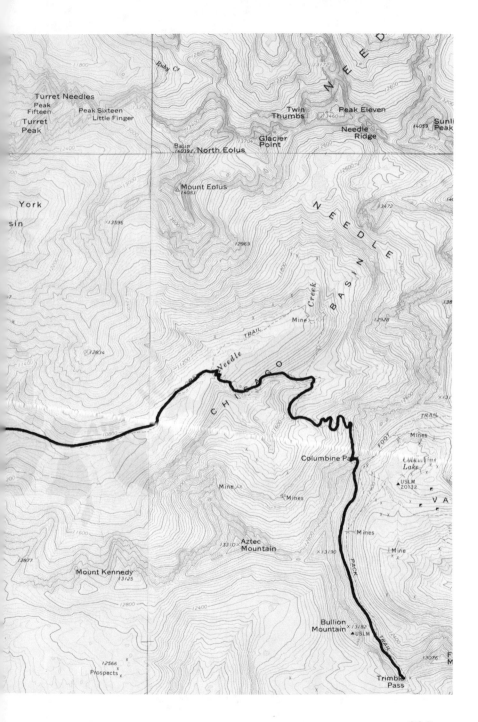

Maps:
7.5 minute Columbine Pass
7.5 minute Mountain View Crest
7.5 minute Snowdon Peak (trailhead area only)
San Juan National Forest

Trimble Pass is in the Weminuche Wilderness. It is just a mile and a half from Columbine Pass, and the two can readily be reached on the same backpacking trip. Trimble Pass is a crossing from Vallecito Basin at the head of Johnson Creek into the Missouri Gulch area to the south.

The best route to Trimble Pass is from Columbine Pass. Follow one of the routes to Columbine Pass (pass number 48). From a trail junction on the east side a few feet down from Columbine Pass, take the fork leading south. The trail south contours for a mile and a half on the east side of a ridge at the head of Vallecito Basin. There is some rocky trail climbing on the final approach to Trimble Pass.

Starting toward Trimble Pass from Columbine Pass.

Approaching Trimble Pass. Columbine Pass is in the distance.

Vallecito Basin from Jupiter Mountain. Columbine Pass is in the right center and Trimble Pass is at the upper left.

Florida Mountain is to the east and Bullion Mountain to the northwest of Trimble Pass. Mount Valois can be seen along the ridge southeast of Florida Mountain. Lillie Lake is in the foreground in the valley southeast. Walk a few yards south of Trimble Pass for a look across Silver Mesa, which extends south. This mesa is east of Missouri Gulch and west of Florida River.

50. Gunsight Pass

Elevation: 12,180 feet
Hiking distance: 15 miles
Starting elevation: 10,140 feet
Elevation gain: 2,400 feet
Rating: moderate
Estimated time: 9½ hours

Maps:
7.5 minute Platoro
7.5 minute Summit Peak
Rio Grande National Forest

Gunsight Pass is the southernmost named pass along the Continental Divide in Colorado. It is in a remote area, and a long drive off the main highways is required to reach the trailhead. You will make a pleasant trail hike in the South San Juan Wilderness before you leave the trail to climb to the pass. The Continental Divide itself is so rugged in this area that the Continental Divide Trail goes below the pass on the east. No trail crosses the divide through Gunsight Pass; therefore, some off-trail hiking is needed to reach the pass.

Drive toward the small town of Platoro, which is southwest of Monte Vista in southern Colorado. There are

Conejos Falls.

Gunsight Pass.

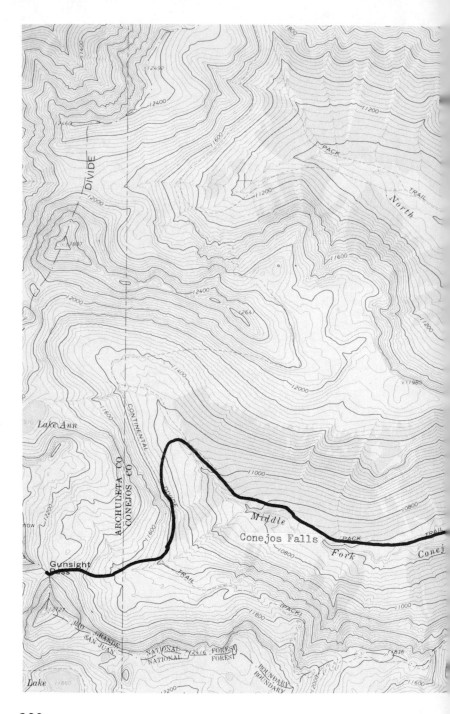

FOREST

River

Conejos

Three Forks

Conejos

River

River

11032

El

Rito

Azul

PACK

TRAIL

Con

The Continental Divide ridge extending east from Gunsight Pass.

various approaches to this area from US 160, Colorado 15, and Colorado 17, all of which are long drives on unpaved roads. From the road west of Platoro, between Platoro and Stunner Pass, take a road southwest to Platoro Reservoir. Follow this road six miles to the trailhead at the road's end. Drive southwest along the northwest side of the reservoir. The trailhead parking area is near the wilderness boundary about two miles beyond the end of the reservoir.

Hike on the trail to the south, as it follows along the west side of the Conejos River. In about two miles, with little change in elevation, you reach a large meadow area called Three Forks. The route to Gunsight Pass follows a trail up Middle Fork Conejos River. Bear to the right where a left-forking trail to Blue Lake goes up a tributary called El Rito Azul. A half mile farther, take the trail to the left across the stream at a junction where the route straight ahead leads up North Fork Conejos River.

Follow the trail south along the right side of Middle Fork Conejos River. As the trail bears west and enters an open area, you get the first view of Gunsight Pass. The trail climbs gradually to the west for the next two miles. Conejos Falls is left of the trail after you reenter the timber, at about 10,600 feet. The falls is not visible from the trail— you must leave the trail and walk to the edge of the canyon. Return to the trail and continue past a drainage coming down from Gunsight Pass.

Soon after the trail leaves the timber, at an elevation of about 11,200 feet, leave the trail to the left. Cross Middle Fork Conejos River and climb the open slope to the southwest. About two hundred feet of climbing will bring you to the Continental Divide Trail, which runs northwest-southwest at the point where you intersect it. Turn left and follow it south about a half mile around the nose of a ridge. Gunsight Pass is on the divide a mile west and some eight hundred feet higher than the Continental Divide Trail.

The route is cross-country from the Continental Divide Trail. Starting south of a patch of timber and near where the trail crosses a drainage, leave the trail on the right and climb directly west. The route follows tundra slopes and then becomes rocky as you near the pass.

Broad, rocky Gunsight Pass must represent a large gun. The pass is a flat area fully two hundred yards between the cliffs on each side. This is quite a contrast with the narrow opening of the Gunsight Pass on Fossil Ridge.

Appendix 1
Tabulation of Colorado Passes
11,000 Feet and Above

The table in this appendix shows data on all the named passes in Colorado that are eleven thousand feet and above. These passes are listed in order of elevation.

Simply stated, a pass is a low point over a ridge between two higher points. There are literally thousands of such passes in the Colorado mountains. Therefore, for the purpose of compiling this list of the highest passes in the state, we include only the officially named ones. These are taken to be the passes with names accepted by the United States Board on Geographic Names. Almost all of the officially named passes have their names printed on the latest United States Geological Survey topographic maps. A few others have names that have been approved by the United States Board on Geographic Names since the last topographic maps were issued.

For some passes, an exact elevation has been measured and is shown on the USGS topographic map. However, the elevation of most passes has not been measured exactly. For such passes, it is necessary to estimate an elevation. This is done by interpolating an elevation from the contour lines on the latest topographic map. In such cases, it is assumed that the elevation is the midpoint between the two contour lines that enclose the pass. For example, if a pass is above the 12,000-foot contour line but below the 12,040 contour, its elevation is listed as 12,020 feet.

For almost all passes served by road or trail, the crossing is at or very near the low point on the ridge. However, there are a few passes where the terrain required the road or trail to cross the ridge at a substantially higher point. In such cases, the elevation of the pass is taken at the point of the road or trail crossing. The most striking example of a crossing higher than the low point on the ridge is Electric Pass, the highest named pass in Colorado.

In compiling the list of passes by elevation, we have found numerous differences from elevations listed in other sources. One reason for these differences is that our compilation is based on the latest USGS topographic maps, including preliminary bluelines. Older maps may have shown different elevations. Another reason for differences is that some sources may have used approximate elevations. Only when arranging passes in exact order of elevation, as we have done in this book, is it important to show the elevation precisely.

Following the pass name in the table is a column showing the type of crossing. For passes crossed by road, the highway number is shown if the road is a state or US highway. Most other roads are unpaved county or forest service roads. The "4WD" passes ordinarily cannot be reached by passenger car but under optimum conditions are accessible by a four-wheel-drive vehicle. All other passes are indicated as being served by "trail" or "no trail." The route indicated in this column is the most difficult portion that must be negotiated. Thus, a route that is partly passenger car road and partly four-wheel-drive road is listed as "4WD." A route that is partly trail and partly off trail is listed as "no trail."

Besides changes in the roadway itself, the classification of a route as being accessible by passenger car or by four-wheel-drive vehicle is a very subjective judgment. We have used just the two categories of vehicle in making this classification—"passenger car" and "4WD." However, there is a wide range of vehicles between the largest passenger cars and those with four-wheel drive. Thus, many smaller cars, trucks, and older cars that drivers don't mind punishing may be able to negotiate routes that we list as "4WD."

The net effect of all these variables results in the listings of passes accessible by automobile being very unscientific and possibly subject to debate. However, we hope that the listings by classification will be a starting point for many people to explore these routes for themselves and thus enjoy the experiences of traveling to the high passes.

In classifying passes as ones that can be reached by passenger car, by four-wheel-drive vehicle, or that require hiking, we have not mentioned those that can be reached by two-wheeled vehicles or on horseback. In general, most of the trail routes to passes can be negotiated by trail bikes or motorcycles in areas where these vehicles are permitted.

The distinction between "trail" and "no trail" also is often fuzzy. In general, we list a route as having a trail if the trail can be followed readily. Those listed as "no trail" usually require some route-finding skills.

The fourth column shows the county in which the pass is located. The fifth column shows the national forest, if any, in which the pass may be found. Some passes are in Rocky Mountain National Park (RMNP). Note in these two columns that many passes are on a dividing line between counties or between national forests, and thus two counties or two national forests are listed.

The last column indicates the U.S. Geological Survey 7.5 minute map on which the pass is located.

Elevation	Name	Route	County	National Forest	Topographic Map
13,500	Electric Pass	trail	Pitkin	White River	Hayden Peak
13,220	Elkhead Pass	trail	Chaffee	San Isabel	Mount Harvard
13,207	Argentine Pass	trail	Clear Creek-Summit	Arapaho	Grays Peak
13,186	Mosquito Pass	4WD	Lake-Park	—	Climax
13,140	The Keyhole	trail	Larimer	RMNP	Longs Peak
13,114	Imogene Pass	4WD	Ouray-San Miguel	Uncompahgre	Ironton
13,020	Hermit Pass	4WD	Custer-Saguache	Rio Grande-San Isabel	Rito Alto Peak
12,980	Blue Lake Pass	trail	Ouray	Uncompahgre	Telluride
12,900	Denver Pass	no trail	Hinsdale-San Juan	—	Handies Peak
12,900	Triangle Pass	trail	Gunnison-Pitkin	Gunnison-White River	Gothic
12,860	Trimble Pass	trail	La Plata	San Juan	Columbine Pass
12,780	Conundrum Pass	no trail	Pitkin	White River	Maroon Bells
12,780	Engineer Pass	4WD	Hinsdale-Ouray	—	Handies Peak
12,780	Sunnyside Saddle	trail	San Juan	—	Handies Peak
12,780	Venable Pass	trail	Saguache	Rio Grande-San Isabel	Rito Alto Peak
12,740	Coffeepot Pass	no trail	Gunnison-Pitkin	Gunnison-White River	Gothic
12,705	Pearl Pass	4WD	Gunnison-Pitkin	Gunnison-White River	Pearl Pass
12,700	Columbine Pass	trail	La Plata	San Juan	Columbine Pass
12,700	Heckert Pass	no trail	Pitkin	White River	Capitol Peak
12,657	Richmond Pass	no trail	Ouray	Uncompahgre	Ironton
12,620	Cinnamon Pass	4WD	Hinsdale-San Juan	—	Handies Peak
12,588	Stony Pass	4WD	San Juan	Rio Grande-San Juan	Howardsville
12,580	Copper Pass	trail	Gunnison-Pitkin	Gunnison-White River	Gothic
12,580	Fall Creek Pass	trail	Eagle	White River	Mt. of the Holy Cross
12,580	Willow Pass	trail	Pitkin	White River	Maroon Bells

Elevation	Name	Route	County	National Forest	Topographic Map
12,541	Pawnee Pass	trail	Boulder-Grand	Arapaho-Roosevelt	Monarch Lake
12,540	Whiskey Pass	no trail	Costilla	—	El Valle Creek
12,500	Halfmoon Pass	trail	Mineral-Saguache	Rio Grande	Halfmoon Pass
12,500	Stone Man Pass	no trail	Boulder-Grand	RMNP	McHenrys Peak
12,500	West Maroon Pass	trail	Pitkin	White River	Maroon Bells
12,493	Hunchback Pass	trail	San Juan	Rio Grande-San Juan	Storm King Peak
12,462	Buckskin Pass	trail	Pitkin	White River	Maroon Bells
12,460	Storm Pass	trail	Gunnison	Gunnison	West Elk Peak
12,453	Jones Pass	road	Clear Creek-Grand	Arapaho	Byers Peak
12,420	Cony Pass	no trail	Boulder	RMNP	Isolation Peak
12,420	Trail Rider Pass	trail	Gunnison-Pitkin	Gunnison-White River	Snowmass Mountain
12,398	The Saddle	trail	Larimer	RMNP	Trail Ridge
12,380	Fancy Pass	trail	Eagle	White River	Mount Jackson
12,380	Frigid Air Pass	trail	Pitkin	White River	Snowmass Mountain
12,220	Lake Pass	trail	Chaffee-Gunnison	Gunnison-San Isabel	Pieplant
12,180	Gunsight Pass	no trail	Archuleta	Rio Grande-San Juan	Summit Peak
12,180	Ptarmigan Pass	trail	Grand-Larimer	RMNP	McHenrys Peak
12,167	Gunsight Pass	trail	Gunnison	Gunnison	Fairview Peak
12,159	Black Powder Pass	no trail	Park-Summit	Arapaho-Pike	Boreas Pass
12,154	Tincup Pass	4WD	Chaffee-Gunnison	Gunnison-San Isabel	Cumberland Pass
12,140	Chalk Creek Pass	trail	Chaffee	San Isabel	Garfield
12,140	Hancock Pass	4WD	Chaffee-Gunnison	Gunnison-San Isabel	Garfield
12,126	Cottonwood Pass	road	Chaffee-Gunnison	Gunnison-San Isabel	Tincup
12,120	Webster Pass	4WD	Park-Summit	Arapaho-Pike	Montezuma
12,100	Avalanche Pass	trail	Gunnison	White River	Marble

Elevation	Name	Route	County	National Forest	Topographic Map
12,100	Granite Pass	trail	Larimer	RMNP	Longs Peak
12,093	Independence Pass	road-Colo 93	Lake-Pitkin	San Isabel-White River	Independence Pass
12,090	Gunsight Pass	4WD	Gunnison	Gunnison	Oh-be-joyful
12,061	Boulder-Grand Pass	no trail	Boulder-Grand	RMNP	Isolation Peak
12,046	French Pass	trail	Park-Summit	Arapaho-Pike	Boreas Pass
12,022	Kokomo Pass	no trail	Eagle-Summit	Arapaho-White River	Copper Mountain
12,020	Browns Pass	trail	Chaffee-Gunnison	Gunnison-San Isabel	Mount Yale
12,020	Cumberland Pass	road	Gunnison	Gunnison	Cumberland Pass
12,020	Napoleon Pass	trail	Gunnison	Gunnison	Cumberland Pass
12,020	Searle Pass	no trail	Summit	Arapaho	Copper Mountain
11,990	Loveland Pass	road	Clear Creek-Summit	Arapaho	Loveland Pass
11,980	Andrews Pass	no trail	Grand-Larimer	RMNP	McHenrys Peak
11,980	Angel Pass	trail	Gunnison	Gunnison	Oh-be-joyful
11,980	Tomichi Pass	4WD	Gunnison	Gunnison	Whitepine
11,940	San Luis Pass	trail	Mineral-Saguache	Gunnison-Rio Grande	San Luis Peak
11,928	Taylor Pass	4WD	Gunnison-Pitkin	Gunnison-White River	Hayden Peak
11,925	Hagerman Pass	4WD	Lake-Pitkin	San Isabel-White River	Homestake Reservoir
11,921	Weston Pass	road	Lake-Park	Pike-San Isabel	Mount Sherman
11,906	Arapaho Pass	trail	Boulder-Grand	Arapaho-Roosevelt	Monarch Lake
11,900	Eccles Pass	trail	Summit	Arapaho	Vail Pass
11,900	Puerto Blanco	trail	Mineral	San Juan	Palomino Mountain
11,900	Uneva Pass	trail	Summit	Arapaho	Vail Pass
11,860	Icefield Pass	no trail	Larimer	RMNP	Comanche Peak
11,860	Rogers Pass	4WD	Gilpin-Grand	Arapaho-Roosevelt	Empire
11,841	Midway Pass	trail	Pitkin	White River	Thimble Rock
11,840	South Fork Pass	trail	Pitkin	White River	Mt. Champion
11,837	Buchanan Pass	trail	Boulder-Grand	Arapaho-Roosevelt	Isolation Peak
11,827	Iceberg Pass	road-US 34	Larimer	RMNP	Trail Ridge
11,820	East Maroon Pass	trail	Gunnison-Pitkin	Gunnison-White River	Maroon Bells
11,796	Fall River Pass	road—US 34	Larimer	RMNP	Fall River Pass
11,789	Ophir Pass	4WD	San Juan-San Miguel		

Elevation	Name	Route	County	National Forest	Topographic Map
11,780	Caribou Pass	trail	Grand	Arapaho	Monarch Lake
11,780	Eagle Pass	4WD	La Plata	San Juan	La Plata
11,780	Summit Pass	trail	Rio Grande	Rio Grande-San Juan	Elwood Pass
11,777	Ptarmigan Pass	trail	Grand-Summit	Arapaho	Dillon
11,766	Williams Pass	4WD	Chaffee-Gunnison	Gunnison-San Isabel	Cumberland Pass
11,765	Ptarmigan Pass	4WD	Eagle-Summit	Arapaho-White River	Pando
11,747	Devils Thumb Pass	trail	Boulder-Grand	Arapaho-Roosevelt	East Portal
11,740	Blowout Pass	4WD	Rio Grande	Rio Grande	Jasper
11,740	Kennebec Pass	4WD	La Plata	San Juan	La Plata
11,740	Oh-be-joyful Pass	trail	Gunnison	Gunnison	Oh-be-joyful
11,740	Red Buffalo Pass	trail	Eagle-Summit	Arapaho-White River	Vail Pass
11,720	Treasure Pass	trail	Mineral	Rio Grande-San Juan	Wolf Creek Pass
11,740	Sprague Pass	no trail	Grand-Larimer	RMNP	McHenrys Peak
11,700	Vasquez Pass	no trail	Clear Creek-Grand	Arapaho	Berthoud Pass
11,700	Yule Pass	trail	Gunnison	Gunnison-White River	Snowmass Mountain
11,671	Rollins Pass	road	Boulder-Grand	Arapaho-Roosevelt	East Portal
11,669	Guanella Pass	road	Clear Creek	Arapaho-Pike	Mount Evans
11,660	Stormy Peaks Pass	trail	Larimer	RMNP	Pingree Park
11,660	Mandall Pass	trail	Garfield	Routt	Devils Causeway
11,631	Elwood Pass	road	Rio Grande	Rio Grande-San Juan	Elwood Pass
11,620	Daisy Pass	trail	Gunnison	Gunnison	Oh-be-joyful
11,620	Flint Pass	no trail	Larimer	RMNP	Comanche Peak
11,620	Half Moon Pass	trail	Eagle	White River	Mt. of the Holy Cross
11,585	Georgia Pass	road	Park-Summit	Arapaho-Pike	Boreas Pass
11,540	Red Dirt Pass	trail	Jackson-Routt	Routt	Mount Zirkel
11,539	Hoosier Pass	road-Colo 9	Park-Summit	Arapaho-Pike	Alma
11,532	Saint Louis Pass	trail	Grand	Arapaho	Byers Peak
11,484	Timberline Pass	trail	Larimer	RMNP	Trail Ridge
11,481	Boreas Pass	road	Park-Summit	Arapaho-Pike	Boreas Pass

Elevation	Name	Route	County	National Forest	Topographic Map
11,476	Bowen Pass	trail	Grand-Jackson	Arapaho-Routt	Bowen Mountain
11,420	Piedra Pass	trail	Mineral	Rio Grande-San Juan	Palomino Mountain
11,380	Music Pass	trail	Custer-Saguache	Rio Grande-San Isabel	Crestone Peak
11,380	Old Monarch Pass	road	Chaffee-Gunnison	Gunnison-San Isabel	Pahlone Peak
11,372	Browns Pass	4WD	Park	Pike	Fairplay West
11,340	Fremont Pass	road-Colo 91	Lake	San Isabel	Climax
11,331	Thunder Pass	trail	Grand-Jackson	RMNP-Routt	Fall River Pass
11,315	Berthoud Pass	road-US 40	Clear Creek-Grand	Arapaho	Berthoud Pass
11,300	Bottle Pass	no trail	Grand	Arapaho	Bottle Pass
11,300	Forest Canyon Pass	trail	Larimer	RMNP	Fall River Pass
11,300	Monarch Pass	road-US 50	Chaffee-Gunnison	Gunnison-San Isabel	Pahlone Peak
11,300	Slumgullion Pass	road	Hinsdale	Gunnison	Slumgullion Pass
11,260	Bonito Pass	trail	Rio Grande	Rio Grande-San Juan	Elwood Pass
11,260	Mummy Pass	trail	Larimer	RMNP	Comanche Peak
11,253	Baker Pass	trail	Grand-Jackson	Arapaho-Routt	Mount Richthofen
11,248	Cordova Pass	road	Huerfano-Las Animas	San Isabel	Cucharas Pass
11,220	Bolam Pass	4WD	Dolores-San Juan	San Juan	Hermosa Peak
11,220	Grassy Pass	trail	Larimer	Roosevelt	Rawah Lakes
11,220	Squaw Pass	trail	Hinsdale	Rio Grande-San Juan	Cimarrona Peak
11,140	Chapin Pass	trail	Larimer	RMNP	Trail Ridge
11,140	Puzzle Pass	no trail	La Plata	San Juan	La Plata
11,100	Red Mountain Pass	road-US 550	Ouray-San Juan	Uncompahgre	Ironton
11,089	Shrine Pass	road	Eagle-Summit	Arapaho-White River	Vail Pass
11,060	Riflesight Notch	road	Grand	Arapaho	East Portal
11,057	Castle Pass	trail	Gunnison	Gunnison	Anthracite Range
11,020	Juniper Pass	road-Colo 103	Clear Creek	Arapaho	Idaho Springs
11,020	Monument Pass	no trail	Gunnison-Ouray	Uncompahgre	Washboard Rock
11,020	Slagle Pass	no trail	Gunnison-Ouray	—	Buckhorn Lakes
11,020	Milk Cow Pass	road	Saguache	Rio Grande	Pine Cone Knob

Appendix 2
Colorado Passes 12,000 Feet and Above Not Covered in the Hiking Guide

Mosquito Pass (13,186 feet) is a popular four-wheel-drive crossing of the Mosquito Range between Leadville and Fairplay.

Imogene Pass (13,114 feet) is crossed by a rugged four-wheel-drive road between Ouray and Telluride.

Hermit Pass (13,020 feet) in the Sangre de Cristo Range can be reached from the east by a four-wheel-drive road west of Westcliffe. The west-side approach to Hermit Pass is by trail.

Engineer Pass (12,780 feet) is a frequently used four-wheel-drive crossing in the San Juan Mountains between Lake City and Ouray or Silverton.

Pearl Pass (12,705 feet) is a rugged four-wheel-drive crossing of the crest of the Elk Mountains between Aspen and Crested Butte.

Cinnamon Pass (12,620 feet) in the San Juan Mountains is a four-wheel-drive crossing between Lake City and Ouray or Silverton.

Stony Pass (12,588 feet) is a crossing in the San Juan Mountains used for long four-wheel-drive trips from Silverton to Rio Grande Reservoir.

Whiskey Pass (12,540 feet) is a crossing of the Culebra Range in southern Colorado. A four-wheel-drive approach on the west side leads to an abandoned tunnel below the pass. This area is on private property and currently requires payment of an access fee.

Jones Pass (12,453 feet) can be reached on the east side by passenger car from US 40 between Interstate 70 and Berthoud Pass. The road descends a short distance down the west side from Jones Pass, but there is no vehicle access from the west.

Tincup Pass (12,154 feet) is a four-wheel-drive crossing of the Continental Divide in the southern Sawatch Range between St. Elmo and Tincup.

Hancock Pass (12,140 feet) is a four-wheel-drive Continental Divide crossing of the southern Sawatch Range between Hancock and Pitkin.

Cottonwood Pass (12,126 feet) is a passenger-car crossing of the Continental Divide between Buena Vista and Taylor Park.

Webster Pass (12,120 feet) is a crossing of the Continental Divide from Montezuma on good four-wheel-drive road with rougher descents to the east down Handcart Gulch or over Red Cone.

Independence Pass (12,093 feet) is a paved-road crossing of the Continental Divide between Aspen and US 24 between Buena Vista and Leadville.

Gunsight Pass (12,090 feet) may be reached on the north side by four-wheel-drive vehicle from the Slate River road north of Crested Butte. There is no access from the south side of the pass.

Cumberland Pass (12,020 feet) is crossed by a passenger-car road between Taylor Park and Pitkin.

Appendix 3
Some High Passes with Unofficial Names

Besides the passes with official names, there are many passes in Colorado that are known by unofficial names. Such names are not shown on the United States Geological Survey topographic maps and have not been approved by the United States Board on Geographic Names. However, such unofficial names often are used in reference books and may be common in local usage. Consequently, many of the passes with unofficial names are better known than some passes with official names.

Here are some of the passes above twelve thousand feet with unofficial names:

Horseshoe Pass (13,180 feet) is a trail crossing of the Mosquito Range crest between Horseshoe Mountain and Mount Sheridan.

Twin Thumbs Pass (13,060 feet) is in the Weminuche Wilderness. It is the best crossing from Chicago Basin to the upper Noname Creek basin. There is no constructed trail for this difficult crossing.

Dyke Col (13,060 feet) is on the ridge east of Mount Sneffels. The crossing between Cirque Mountain and Kismet is a non-trail route from Yankee Boy Basin into Blaine Basin.

Knife Point Pass (12,860 feet) is a steep crossing without trail between Jagged Mountain and Knife Point in the Weminuche Wilderness. It is between the Noname Creek basin and the Vallecito Creek valley.

Red Mountain Pass (12,860 feet) is a Continental Divide crossing south of Red Mountain in the Sawatch Range. It was once crossed by a wagon road that mostly has disappeared on the western side.

Black Bear Pass (12,840) is a high ridge crossing between Ouray and Telluride. It is such a rugged four-wheel-drive road that some rental firms will not permit drivers to try Black Bear Pass.

Lost Man Pass (12,820 feet) is a trail crossing above Lost Man Lake in the Sawatch Range near Independence Pass.

Grizzly Pass (12,760 feet) is a Continental Divide crossing in the vicinity of Loveland Pass in the Front Range. It's at the head of Grizzly Gulch, but there's no road or trail over it. It became known as Grizzly Pass when it was once considered as a possible road crossing.

Pomeroy Pass (12,740 feet) is a trail crossing from North Fork Arkansas River to the Chalk Creek area. The trail has not been maintained, and portions of it are obscure.

Yvonne Pass (12,740 feet) is a four-wheel-drive crossing between Ouray or Silverton and Lake City. The pass is on the opposite side of Engineer Mountain from Engineer Pass.

Ute Pass (12,702 feet) is crossed by a trail in the Weminuche Wilderness. It is near the Continental Divide east of Hunchback Pass.

Comanche Pass (12,700 feet) is a trail crossing of the Sangre de Cristo Range. It is just south of Venable Pass, and the two can be combined on excellent loop trips.

Wildhorse Creek Pass (12,660 feet) is a trail crossing west of Wildhorse Peak. The trail is from the American Flats area near Engineer Pass to the valley north of Ouray.

Calico Pass (12,540 feet) is a crossing in the southern part of the Sawatch Range. From Grizzly Gulch south of St. Elmo, a trail that has now largely disappeared once led into the Cyclone Creek drainage to the south.

Nebo Pass (12,460 feet) is a trail crossing of the Continental Divide in the Weminuche Wilderness just south of Hunchback Pass.

New York Pass (12,460 feet) is in the Sawatch Range west of Independence Pass. It is a crossing from the New York Creek drainage on the north to the Pine Creek valley to the south.

Bear Creek Pass (12,445 feet) is a ridge crossing on good trail in the area northwest of Silverton. The route is between the South Mineral Creek valley and Lake Hope in the valley of Lake Fork.

Gunsight Pass (12,380 feet) is one of several Colorado passes that have been given this name. This one is crossed by a trail in the Weminuche Wilderness in the area southwest of Rio Grande Pyramid.

216

Central Pass (12,340 feet) is a crossing of the crest of the Gore Range. The off-trail route over this pass is from the North Rock Creek drainage on the east to the Bighorn Creek valley on the west.

Bowman Pass (12,241 feet) is in the Sawatch Range near New York Pass. It is crossed by a trail from Bowman Creek north to the Bruin Creek drainage.

Index